An(

Heathenism: Modern Philosophies, Concepts, Views

© Andreas Mang
Eigenverlag Andreas Mang
(independent publisher)
1st and ∞th edition 2014

Translation of the German original "Aufgeklärtes Heidentum",
(ISBN 978-1479279944)

Cover photo/design:
Axel Voss, http://www.symbology.de/

ISBN: 978-1502400338

Heathenism:
Modern Philosophies, Concepts, Views

TABLE OF CONTENTS

Preface to the English Translation 7
Introduction 9
What Is Religion? 15
What Is Faith? 25
What Is a Myth? 31
What Is a God? 49
What Is Atheism? 63
What Is a Sacrifice? 71
What Is Magic? 79
What Awaits Us After Death? 89
Why I Am a Heathen. 103
Appendix – Right-wing Extremism and 3rd Reich 139
Bibliography 157
List of Tables and Figures 169
Index 171

PREFACE TO THE ENGLISH TRANSLATION

This is a translation of a book I wrote in German roughly two years ago. It is written from a more or less German perspective and may therefore contain a lot of things that make only sense if you know the German background. If some words or phrases were not translatable into English very well or not at all, I tried to explain in the text what was really meant. If I have failed to notice hardly translatable text passages, please do not wonder what strange things are written down there.

In the German language a German (*Germane*) is no one living today but refers to the ancient tribes. If "Germanic" is stated here in this book, it means ancient Germanic or Teutonic.

A slight confusion may arise about the way I spelled "god". Whenever I needed a simple and superficial labelling for divine entities, I just wrote "god" in lower-case. As a name, e.g. for the Christian God, or when referring to a specific pantheon I used the upper-case variant. In other words, "a god" or "gods" denotes a semantic category, "God" means a specific god named God and "Gods" refers to the Gods in a more respectful way. In the German language every noun starts with a capital letter, so this distinction is not possible and thus does not occur in the original book.

I published the original book and am going to publish this one myself using a books-on-demand service. It is a completely private project without a budget for a professional translation. I did all the translation myself. Thus this book may sound less sophisticated or eloquent as originally intended. A lot of the quoted German literature has proper and professional translations on the market. Actually I was often too lazy to seek them out and translated most of that myself as well.

The same may apply for a lot of names of mythological entities or places. I tried to use the proper English designations, but if you encounter a name looking a bit unfamiliar, it may be the German version of it.

I made use of all the supplies modern information technology can provide and had some help from friends and native speakers, who enriched my vocabulary and did the proof-reading. If you still find errors and sentences that sound totally weird or silly in English – it is entirely my fault.

My sincere thanks to Penda Ullrsson who provided more help on this English edition than I could hope for or would ever be entitled to ask for.

Andreas Mang, September 2014

INTRODUCTION

If you were to tell anyone you are a heathen or pagan, you will likely be confronted with misunderstanding and prejudice. It is totally unimportant whether your dialogue partner is a Christian, some other monotheist, or an atheist. Here "heathen" is not a synonym for infidel, non-Christian or atheist but denotes followers of one or more pagan religions, namely pre-Christian and within the scope of this book European polytheisms.

In my opinion the main cause of misunderstanding is in the Western world's definitions and meanings of religious concepts such as "faith", "god" and "religion". They all derive from a Christian background and have a partially or completely different meaning in Paganism. Perhaps at the end of the last paragraph the reader has already wondered how someone could follow more than one religion. In Paganism this is no problem, though one often speaks of "different cults" rather than "different religions". Although, due to the fact, that the pantheons of several but in union conducted cults are so different from each other, I regard the categorisation into different religions as permissible.

At first in this book the terms "religion", "faith", "myth" and "god" were described in a way so they fit into Paganism or how they are used in that area respectively. There are great differences in the definition of religion and a god between Paganism and monotheisms like Christianity, Islam and Judaism. Faith and myth have a clearly different meaning and application within a pagan religion.

Then comes a few words on atheism. Not because I want to fight its supposed criticism or opposition to Heathenism but to point out that modern Western atheism, whose philosophical basis was set up in the 19th century, is more an antithesis of Christianity than of religion in general and its criticism is more or less irrelevant in Heathenism. Furthermore that chapter contains some remarks on religious freedom.

Then the topics "sacrifice", "magic" and "afterlife" are laid out, because in the public perception, similar misunderstandings occur just as with the more fundamental and above mentioned areas "religion" and "God".

At this point I would like to clarify that with all my statements I did try to meet a broad consent within the pagan community. Naturally there will be many heathens who will not agree at all with some things I propose here. Especially in the area of "magic" this will take place quite often, because I have a naturalistic world-view and am convinced that nothing we encounter has a supernatural origin.

Philosophy and theology are not empirical science. Personally, in direct comparison to the natural sciences I even do not really consider them to be science at all but treat their content as complex and much elaborated opinions. Their level may be so high, that an academic education is necessary to formulate, to understand and to develop them, but they still remain unprovable views one may follow or decline. To assume or propose an objective or absolute truth is not admissible. Thus I would never support such a thing, and this book has no intention in such a manner.

After all these explanations on pagan terminology I present why the Nordic-Germanic Heathenism appeals me so much as to follow it, though I admire the Graeco-Roman as well.

Connections are often made between the Nordic-Germanic Heathenism and extreme right-wing political opinions and thus the disastrous past of the Third Reich. According to my judgement, since all those activities do not comply with the teachings told in the myths and Paganism had no relevant social role in the Third Reich, as it is sometimes stated, it had no influence whatsoever on my decision to be a heathen. Therefore some supplementing explanation on this topic were written in an appendix.

A few notes on how the references are set up:

References are set up in square brackets and consist of an abbreviation of that work's first mentioned author plus the two-digit release year. If such a reference would not be unique a small letter is added as an index. The reference is sorted by authors' names and release years.

References to websites or other online resources use their title rather than the often missing author's token if necessary. Additionally the timestamp (by month) is recorded in the reference when I last checked its content, because it may change and have been moved somewhere else in the near future or even lately.

Biblical references are put in round brackets and use the common codes. English verses are always taken from the King James Version, Latin from the Vulgate [Bib12].

I would like to emphasise that this book has no missionary or proselytising function, even though a little increase of organised Paganism would certainly be a good thing, as the membership world-wide is statistically insignificant.

The main intention is to set straight the many common misunderstandings about modern and ancient Paganism and to show how and why Heathenism can fascinate people even today. This way, I hope to provide a better insight into this form of religion for practitioners and also for outsiders.

I admit though, that I would be very happy over anyone who extracts from this book some first or additional interest in Paganism or even a wish to practice it. Likewise, I would be happy too if practising heathens received some as yet unidentified thoughts, ideas, or conceptions out of it.

Now I want to thank all the people whose support made this book possible. At first I thank my wife. Without her I would have neither survived a recent serious accident nor enjoyed the beautiful and fulfilled life enabling tasks like writing a book.

Then my parents, whose education and support, including the demanded confirmation, created a solid basis for my present day world-view, which is explained in this book.

Furthermore friends and good acquaintances in real life and the virtual world. Community, co-operation and many discussions with them shaped my various opinions including those, which are important for the topics presented here.

Last but not least, Prof. Dr. Gerald Dyker, who did the first proof-reading and whose requests, questions and ideas led to many additions to the original text.

Περὶ θεῶν λέγε, ὡς εἰσίν.
Speak of the Gods as they are.
(Bias of Priene)

WHAT IS RELIGION?

Are you religious?

Seemingly a simple question but, if asked, I would have enormous problems trying to answer it with either "yes" or "no". If I answered "yes" it would be false, if I answered "no" I would be most likely misunderstood. This is because the current general meaning of the word "religion" comes from a Christian perspective and thus can only apply to religions that are very similar to Christianity or other Abrahamitic monotheisms such as Judaism and Islam.

A common definition of religion is "to be bound to God". I have heard this statement even from pagans who just exchanged "God" with "Gods". This definition was written down in the early 4th century by the North African Christian apologist Lucius Caecilius Firmianus, called Lactantius, who is counted among the Church Fathers. Lactantius derives *religio* from *religare* = "to bind", religion is for him the binding of devotion between men and God [Fir12].

In later times, especially the Middles Ages, religion was regarded as an organised belief in God, Gods or other higher powers. That regard has lasted until the present day. Knaurs' German dictionary defines religion as [Her85]:

"**1** *belief in one or several supernatural powers and its cult*
2 *confession of faith*; Christian, Jewish religion"

In regards to Paganism this definition poses two problems. First, a certain belief or faith plays a different role in Heathenism as implied here (see chapter WHAT IS FAITH?). Second, the phrase "supernatural powers" may easily cause misunderstandings as pagan Gods are usually considered to be immanent, i.e. being part of the cosmos, rather than supernatural in the sense of being transcendent or otherworldly (see chapter WHAT IS A GOD?).

But the real problem is the alleged necessary reference to those supernatural powers. Heathenism is not affected here but regarding Buddhism, for example, the question often arises whether it is a religion at all or "only" a philosophy of life or world-view. Gods or other higher beings are irrelevant in Buddhism. You may believe in them, revere and worship them, but it is not required. Someone who completely dismisses higher powers or beings can be a Buddhist nonetheless. Buddhist temples, monasteries, priests and monks do exist. There is an attitude towards life and a code of conduct which ought to prepare you for the next life or Nirvana. To me there is no doubt that Buddhism is a religion, it just lacks gods as constitutive elements.

According to my viewpoint a far better definition of the term religion was made in pre-Christian times by Cicero [Cic95]. Cicero derives *religio* from *relegere* = "to collect" or "to pick sth. up", in the figurative sense "to recollect". Here, to follow a religion means to adhere to its rituals, its ethics, its values, its ideals and its traditions. To put gods in general or specific Gods or higher beings, no matter in what numbers, into an exactly defined pantheon or to have compulsory or dogmatic views about their qualities is not important. The faith in such constellations is more or less insignificant, there is nothing like a "false belief" or heresy.

In that context Cicero understands something different in the term "superstition" (*superstitio* in the Latin origin). In the present, which has been greatly influenced by Christianity, its usage implies a false belief in false Gods, false powers, or false conceptions. To him *superstitio* is false piety such as excessive praying or sacrificing, an exaggeration of the religion within the way of life, so that the relation between religious and "normal" life becomes unbalanced. The above mentioned Lactantius disagrees firmly with this notion by the way [Fir12].

This definition of the term "religion" avoids the disadvantages of the modern common one. Here even Buddhism counts as a religion without problems or additional assumptions.

In regards to Germanic Heathenism it is interesting how the ancient Germans thought about religion. Unfortunately there is no written legacy comparable to the philosophical works of the Greeks and Romans, thus we lack any knowledge. With respect to the many similarities between Greco-Roman and Germanic mythology I assume the fundamental ideas behind religion did not significantly differ, even though the latter with its Christian influences is not as well preserved as the former, especially since its legacy was compiled during the Middle Ages. I guess the same applies for Celtic and Slavic interpretations of that term.

Many people think that you can only have one religion. To adhere to a religion automatically requires beholding any other as false.

The fact that the majority of the Japanese follows two religions, Buddhism and Shintoism, which have nearly nothing in common, disproves this notion. Buddhism teaches the overcoming of the personal ego and the individuality to avoid continuous rebirth and to enter Nirvana after death. In contrast Shintoism is an animistic natural religion. The souls of the deceased reach a new home in a shrine or somewhere in nature. In Shintoism *kami* (神) , usually translated as "Gods", are revered. This translation is not precise though. A *kami* might as well be a nature spirit or a soul. For an introduction into Shintoism see [Lok01].

In ancient pagan times it was also common to follow more than one religion [Kla95], although today we would call them "cults" rather than religions. But with respect to the above said definition of religion made by Cicero I do not see a significant distinction between a cult and a religion. There is absolutely no difference in conforming to the requirements of two differing religious cults or two separate religions.

Thus a Roman followed the state and the domestic religions at the least. In the state religion the Roman pantheon was revered and in the latter, for example, the household deities *lares* and *penates*. Those beliefs match well and do not contradict each other as Buddhism and Shintoism obviously do to some extent. Religious societies[1] were common in the ancient world as well. They formed after the downfall of the Greek city-States and the mystery cults belonged to them [Kla95]. The Gods of the Isis-cult e.g. do not fit into the Roman pantheon and an association or combination is nearly impossible. For political and ethical reasons (the latter might have had a religious source) the Roman senate interfered repeatedly

---

[1] Interestingly many terms still used in Christianity derive from those ancient religious societies [Kla95], like συνόδος = "gathering" (synod) or from Egyptian cults πρεσβύτεροι = "elders" (presbyters).

with that Egyptian and other cults and even banned them temporarily. Neither their practice nor their expansion could be prevented though [Klo06].

The ostensible inconsistent results of following two religions with incompatible pantheons disappear because the pagan conceptions about the Gods usually differ greatly from the monotheistic ones. If you understand a god to be a human description of something very difficult to describe, a different pantheon is simply a different view of the same constructs behind their imagery. The Romans called it *interpretatio Romana* = "Roman interpretation", when they identified their Gods with those from other cultures. More details on this topic are discussed in the chapter WHAT IS A GOD?.

The properties and "areas of expertise" of the Gods coming from different pantheons and their relations among each other may prevent addressing them together in one ritual or prayer. Switching from the usual pantheon to a different one in another ritual should pose no problem for a heathen.

To deem every religion except your own, which is supposed to hold the absolute truth, as totally wrong is a typical trait of Abrahamitic monotheisms. The Egyptologist and cultural scientist Jan Assmann calls this a part of the "Mosaic distinction" and identifies its occurrence with the change of Judaism from poly- or henotheism to monotheism, see [Ass03] or [Ass07]. A well known indicator for that hypothesis is the first commandment from the Old Testament. It does not claim that "God" is an adorable God or that praising him is a positive deed, it simply says "Thou shalt have no other Gods before me." (Exod 20:3). To honour other Gods is wrong, the truth is within your own God only, the falsehood among all others, and that leads directly to the assumption that only your own religion is true. Today many followers of Abrahamitic religions hold a more tolerant notion than in former times. Since the 2nd Vatican Council the Vatican, for example, has not beheld the Roman Catholic Church (RCC) as the one and only source of their anticipated truth but grants other religions to have parts of that truth even though not at the extent of the RCC [Vat65]. To regard all other religions to be false is still part of that notion but as an offensive argument it is more or less only used in fundamentalist denominations nowadays.

The commandments can be seen as a collection of values and virtues that are followed if one believes in the commanding God. In that case they are not God's orders but attitudes of the believers matching their god-conception. One who honours or believes in a monotheistic god has of course no other gods beside him – that makes no sense. Then the given form of the commandments is not "thou shalt or shalt not ..." but "if you believe in this God you do or omit ...". They then deal with ethics rather than the judiciary. The missing punishments in the Decalogue point into that direction too [Sch95].

Of course followers of religions different to the Abrahamitic ones regard their own views to be true but they do not necessarily and categorically refuse all other religions. Good examples are the above mentioned Japanese who have two, by western standards contradictory, religions.

Many religious views, especially ethical ones and those which apply to the conduct of life, are based on the individual attitude towards life. That attitude is developed within the social environment, parental education, personal experiences and also personal decisions. I think it is obvious that because of the many surrounding influences such an attitude is neither a generally nor exactly deducible form of a scientific process and therefore it lacks an impartial validity. But such an impartial validity has to be anticipated or demanded if a single religion should be the sole right one for all people and is propagated using that claim.

An example for a religious view that correlates strongly with the attitude towards life is the attitude towards fate. Stoics e.g. believe in an ultimate predetermination of one's destiny that can be escaped almost only by suicide according to Seneca [Kla96]. Many Christians, Jews and Muslims show such a sophisticated fatalism too, as they regard fate as the result of the deeds and wishes of an omnipotent and omniscient God in which mere humans cannot interfere. Of course they do not accept suicide as an alternative.

An oppositional position is to fight an upcoming negative fate. You find that in Germanic Paganism, where the Gods are caught in the web of destiny or fate just as humanity. They fight against their badly developing destiny even if that fight will prove to be futile. A good example is the myth of Ragnarok [Poe12]. Even though Odin knows he cannot prevent the threatening doom and his own death, he prepares and arms against that fate and tries to circumvent it. This can be treated as a lesson not to accept an upcoming terrible fate but to fight it. Only if you fight do you have a chance to prevent it. The Greek Gods who often toy with man's destiny are sometimes not immune against it. The death of Zeus' son Sarpedon in the 16th song of the Iliad [Hom09] is often interpreted in that manner.

look up myth

Another common mistake made by a lot of religious people, especially monotheists, is to believe their own religion would explain how the world functions in a scientific sense. This is connected to the alleged objective validity of their own religious texts and includes regarding their own creation or other myths to be historical and factual reports or to think evolution is wrong because of obscure dogmas. There are Christians who postulate that the world is 6000 years old, which is nonsense in the face of geological, astronomical and cosmological evidence but can be calculated using the Old Testament like the Anglican bishop Ussher did [Uss50].

I say he, who wants to know how the cosmos *functions*, should read books on physics, chemistry, or biology. He who wants to have a pictorial and poetic description of how to live in this world, should read a myth. And those who want to experience with passion how the worlds depicted in the myths work, should celebrate a religious ritual. Religion can tell you how to live in this world. That is something that science, especially natural science, cannot do. This has nothing to do with lacking truth but with truths from areas which are only very insufficiently or not at all accessible by natural science such as ethics or the attitude towards life.

A good and well known example of what harm can be done by scientifically interpreted myths is the rejection of the heliocentric system by the Roman Catholic Church. Just recently Galileo Galilei was rehabilitated in this regard. The heliocentric system was already developed in the 3rd century B.C: by Aristarchus of Samos [Sag82], who presumably also proposed the possibility of empirical evidence by the stellar parallax[2]. However it is too small to be observed by the naked eye and without a telescope. Unfortunately nothing of his writings is preserved directly; we know his works only through secondary literature. Therefore, any assumptions of his scientific experiments, presumed, planned, or done, are very vague. Aristarchus may have thought of very distant or indefinitely remote stars, which is the very reason for the missing opportunity to proof the parallax with the naked eye.

The bad thing here is that this theory was not rejected because of missing evidence until the modern era, but because of the content of religious myths that point into a different direction and the dogmatisation of philosophical and astronomical propositions like the Ptolemaic geocentric system. If the scientific evidence is actually established the impression is then more or less automatically created that the involved religious myths are completely wrong, no matter what other teachings on the conduct of lifc e.g. they might provide. Of course such scientific cancellation of scientifically interpreted myths promotes atheisms as a rejection of any religion. Myths should therefore be interpreted differently, not scientifically, as we will see in detail in the chapter WHAT IS A MYTH?.

Another important issue with the definition of religion is the categorisation by types or forms. Usually a distinction between monotheism and polytheism is made, but those categories pose some difficulties. By the naming alone they distinguish between religions with exactly one or several gods. But the essential difference between Abrahamitic monotheisms and European polytheisms is not really the number of gods but how they are beheld.

Furthermore Hinduism does not really fit into this categorisation. With roughly 330 million Gods, it certainly belongs to polytheism but as the Gods are often regarded as incarnations of a single higher spirit, it could be called monotheism [Cot08]. But as this spirit

---

[2] Stellar parallax is a shift in the position of near stars in front of the remaining stellar background because the earth is travelling around the sun, see e.g. [Ree11].

usually contains less personal elements and is seen as a cosmological principle, a common category with the monotheisms of Christianity, Judaism and Islam is also not befitting.

Jan Assmann criticises the use of those categories because they came up in "theological controversies in the 17th and 18th century" and are "completely unsuitable for the description of ancient religions" [Ass03]. How many gods there were was not important, and he counts non-divine other higher beings such as angles, demons or "lower mythology" entities in Paganism too, so that the term monotheism would not be precise even if there was only one god.

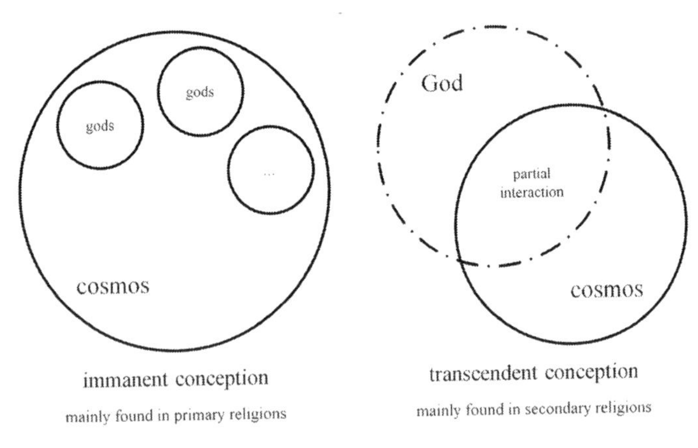

Figure 1: Frequent god-conceptions in primary and secondary religions

Instead Assmann categorises in *primary* and *secondary* religions employing and enhancing the differentiation in primary and secondary religious experiences made by the theologian Theo Sundermeier [Mue87]. Primary religions arose in prehistoric times. We neither know their founder or founders nor the moment of their appearance, probably because they are based on steady development of even older religious views. Of secondary religions we certainly recognise those circumstances. We do know the approximate point in time when they arose and at least one founder. European Paganism and Hinduism are primary in this respect, Christianity, Islam and Buddhism secondary. A historical founder of the monotheistic Judaism is not known, but the time frame when a group of priests did the founding can be narrowed down. Thus Judaism can also be regarded as a secondary religion. Furthermore Assmann points out that every secondary religion is a "book religion", i.e. has some holy scripture, so that the differentiation into book- and non-book-religions is more or less identical. A collection of written down myths and stories without dogmatic or confessing content does not account for a book religion. Therefore that category does not apply to Greek, Roman, or Nordic Heathenism.

Particularly in modern Paganism, the distinction between revelation and experience religions is a common categorisation. This refers rather to the personal dealings with one's own religion than to its external form. A revealed religion is mostly or even completely based on one or more revelations given to one or several founders. This complies with the categories of book religions and of secondary religions. In an experience religion, the personal experiences with the Gods are important, whether in the rite, in prayer, meditation, reflexion on myths, or in other ways such as the reconstruction of older forms of the religion. This distinction is quite apt but causes problems in practice. Christianity e.g. is certainly a revealed religion; its revelation is written down in the Bible. But many Christians behold it as an experience religion, especially regarding the establishment or expansion of a personal relationship with Jesus.

Animistic notions, that almost everything in the world has a spirit or soul, are also present in Paganism, as well as in most other religions. Animism as an archetype of natural religions probably represents one of the very first forms of religion and is therefore inherited to later religions. Funeral rites and ancestor worship connected to notions about an afterlife might also be primarily forms of religion [Rie93].

There are other forms of religious conceptions that are hardly describable with the above-mentioned categories. They have no or only a slight relation to Paganism and its differentiation to Christianity or other Abrahamitic monotheisms, but are mentioned here for completeness.

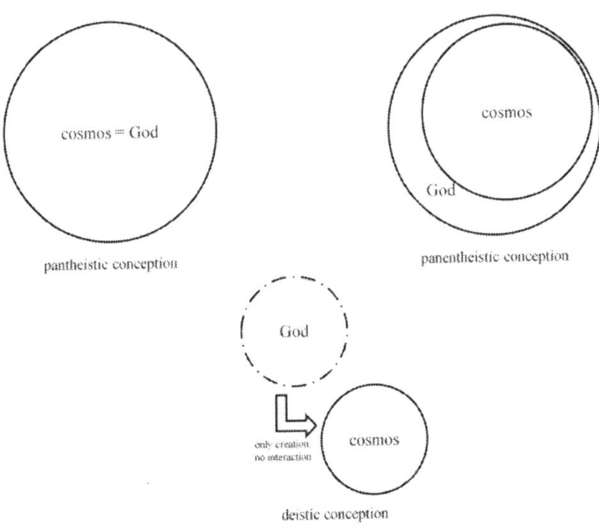

Figure 2: God-conceptions of other religious types

Pantheism: The supposition that the universe and God are identical or that a divine spirit or principle indwells the whole universe.

Panentheism: Like pantheism but here the universe is only a part of a higher being.

Deism: The supposition of a Creator God who does not intervene with the universe at all after the creation.

Pandeism: A mixture of deism and pantheism, i.e. the Maker merges completely into the universe after the creation.

What Is Faith?

Faith, generally speaking, is seen as the basic component of a religion. This is because it represents a key element in Christianity and is conveyed in our public school education and Church teachings such as confirmation classes. Faith is part of the three Christian virtues faith (*fides*), love (*caritas*) and hope (*spes*) (1 Cor 13:13).

Faith does not simply mean to regard something to be true, but usually refers to things whose existence cannot be empirically proven or objectively or logically concluded. In any case it includes desire, love, or approval towards what is believed when the word "believe" is etymologically derived from the Indo-Germanic word *leubh*, which means exactly "to desire", "to love", "to approve", or "to praise" [Gri12].

Of course faith plays a role in European Paganism and other primary religions, but it has a very different significance and relevance as in Christianity or other secondary religions. Values, ethical principles and wisdom expressed in myths are approved as well, but a dogmatic belief in a God or Gods or conception of those gods is not really theologically defined. As seen later in detail in the chapter What Is a God?, there are diverse and partly contradictory god-conceptions especially in modern Heathenism. Here anthropomorphic images of the gods displayed in the myths are the religious basis. Pagans can worship the same Gods together, even if they have different philosophical, theological, or even scientific ideas about them.

I explicitly distinguish between "god-images" and "god-conceptions" which is not found in the literature. A god-image is presented in the respective myths as a figuratively imaginable form. The believer usually knows that is a human image of something different. The widespread view is wrong though, that people, whose religion uses statues and similar images, worshipped those idols instead of the represented Gods.

Now the god-conception describes what is beheld as the basis of the man-made and man-like image. This distinction is important in Paganism, which has fairly clear pictures of the Gods, but a whole range of different ideas about their nature, especially because the latter are not to be believed dogmatically. The religious practices and speech deal with the images, the personal relationship to the Gods or what a monotheist would call faith deals with the concept.

In modern as in ancient Paganism the worship in ritual practices is important; a distinctive faith is more or less secondary. This can already be learned from the writing of Cicero [Cic95], as well as in modern publications. Thus Fritz Steinbock wrote [Ste04]:

> We do not ask: "What do you believe? What do you know? What are you capable of?" We ask: "To which Gods do you sacrifice?"

There are even god-conceptions that require no faith at all, like mine for example. Outsiders or atheists might regard that notion to be nonsensical or dispensable, the pure existence of the Gods itself cannot be neglected though, so here religious faith gives way to a rational definition (see pages 52ff).

That conception is often met with incomprehension. Why sacrifice to or honour a god without being a believer in the traditional sense, is not clear to everybody. Again, the problem is that most people stick to the principles of Christianity, because they are the only ones they know. The significance and the deeper meaning of those basic terms within a religious system cannot be simply applied to a different one. I therefore try to avoid the term "faith" if possible, because it usually evokes false associations. You do not have to regard the anthropomorphic existence of the Gods depicted in the myths as physical reality, if you know or just suppose that the one behind the image or what the image describes exists for real.

The Abrahamitic monotheisms pose an additional problem in which they generally prohibit god-images ("idols") or discourage the believers from using them in practice or as a basis of their faith. In early Judaism this referred to material statues ("graven images") only (Exod 20:4)[3], but later it was extended to intellectual images.

---

[3] In the Christian culture and arts there are common and well known exceptions, see the Sistine Chapel.

Their belief must refer to dogmatised and theological concepts of God; deviations of those concepts quickly lead to new denominations, as the believers with different ideas about their God can hardly join in a rite or a community. Christianity provides a good example. Different conceptions about the connection between God the Father and Jesus lead to disputes and conflicts; the Trinitarian concept won over Arianism only after the First Council of Nicaea in 325 A.D. Besides the Trinity and Arianism there was and there still is Nestorianism, Miaphysitism and only the Gods may know what else.

Interestingly, the Trinity model appears in the entire Indo-European culture. There are various triads of Gods, although the non-Christian ones relate to multiple Gods rather than only one. In Hinduism Brahma, Vishnu and Shiva form the Trimurti (त्रिमूर्ति = Sanskrit "three forms"), in Greek Paganism there is the triad Zeus, Poseidon and Hades, in the Roman Jupiter, Juno and Minerva, in the Germanic Woden, Wili and We (also called Odin, Vili, Ve, but the alliteration is more pleasing). In all of them the three Fates appear, the Moirai, the Parcae, or the Norns . The cult of Isis, as practised in the Roman empire, had Isis, Osiris and Horus.

The theologian Rudolf Bultmann wrote that "not knowledge (γνῶσις) but faith (πίστις)" was characteristic of Christianity [Bul98]. This distinction makes an essential difference between primary and secondary religions. If you follow a revealed or book religion you should or must *believe* what is described in the according revelation or book. Nowadays most believers concentrate on certain key doctrines and ignore issues that contradict current scientific knowledge. But there are also many believers who interpret their scripture literally and consequently reject any deviation from the written word.

The case is different with experience religions and "religion" defined as compliance with the associated rituals, values and traditions rather than faith. Here you rarely find people who take the contents of the myths for literal or historical facts. Spiritual experiences and insights are gained by practice, in rites, meditation, or by other means and not only by reading scripture, even though reading and reflecting on the myths play a big role as well.

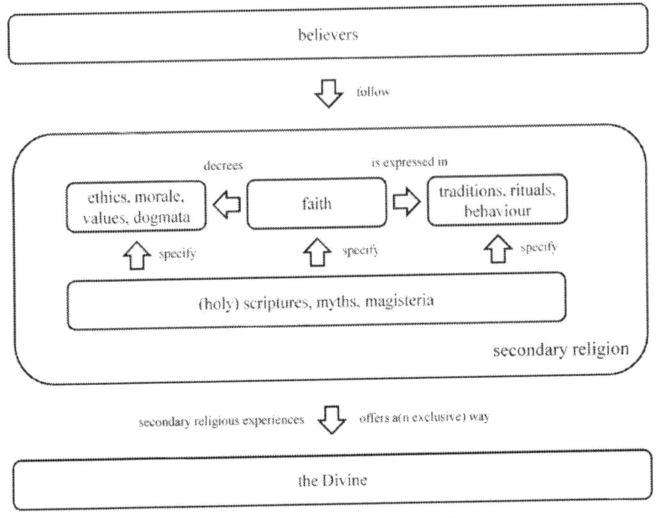

Figure 3: Setting of a secondary religion

This difference can also be seen in the creed, which has a high significance in Christianity and Islam, and must often be memorised and testified at least once in your life. According to www.hagalil.com there is a Jewish creed too [Hag12], its relevance and spreading is however beyond my knowledge.

Heathenism has a different stance here. There may be more, but I personally know only one pagan community having an official creed, the Danish *Forn Siðr* = "the old custom". They refer to the so-called *trosbekendelse* as a "poetic definition of faith and world-view" [For12], and as far as I am informed, it has been made official only because that is necessary for the governmental acknowledgement of a religious community in Denmark. That necessity is probably in alignment with the views of the Lutheran State church.

Contrary to what is presumed for all religions by most people in the Western world, there are definitely religions, in which no commitment to a written creed and thus to a written faith and belief is necessary or even important. Unfortunately, it is incredibly hard to explain to those people how someone can worship Gods without believing in the traditional Christian sense. For them, a concrete and precisely defined faith is a prerequisite for worship.

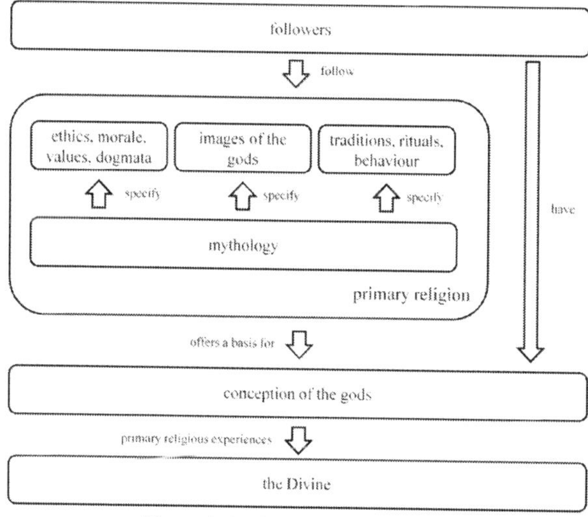

Figure 4: Setting of a primary religion

In my opinion a commitment to one's own written scriptural faith is also related to the possible number of simultaneously practised or followed religions. This was already addressed in the last chapter. A well-defined belief, which is connected to an alleged absolute truth, almost automatically requires that you cannot accept further religions in addition to your own.

If there is no such connection of absolute truth and dogmatic statements, it is no problem to follow multiple and even ostensibly contradictory religions such as the Japanese do, for example, with Buddhism and Shintoism.

Nowadays, it is often stated, that the Romans pursued the Christians because of their "false" faith. If someone thinks of faith within only a certain conception of a god and it represents the crux of the truth, it is an understandable conclusion to view non-followers as opponents because of their different faith. But as we can see from the previously shown ancient definition of religion, with the broad non-existence of creeds in Paganism, and the actual practice of many non-Roman religions in Rome, a presumed false faith could hardly be the reason for persecution.

The heathen Roman Empire was endowed with a certain religious freedom which, however, was not as liberal as today. But in contrast to the later Christian era, where in fact every other religion was forbidden, other cults and religions could be followed. Bans or persecutions were either politically motivated or came from the distrust towards cult practised in secret. The Dionysus and the Isis cult were prohibited by the Senate several times [Klo06], the former was even pursued extremely brutal in 186 B.C. after the so-called "Bacchantes scandal" with 7,000 estimated casualties.

A political reason for the persecution of a religion was the rejection of the State cult, and later of the emperor cult. The public practice of these two cults expressed the accepted affiliation with the Roman Empire. Christians rejected both for reasons of faith, which raised suspicions as it was viewed as political opposition. How rumours of strange rites, perhaps practised in secret, played a role here, is hard to say. I think it is possible and likely that reports on the celebration of the Eucharist, in which Christians seemingly ate the flesh of their master and drank his blood, may have led to some suspicion on the ethics and moral stance of the new cult.

Anyway, due to the missing empirical research possibilities on god-conceptions I think it is pointless to propose and preach general or even absolute truths in religion, like the Abrahamitic monotheisms usually do.

A very appropriate statement on faith and truth in the field of religion, which I agree with wholeheartedly, was made by Siddhartha Gautama, the founder of Buddhism [Gau93]: "Do not believe just because you have heard it. Do not believe in traditions simply because they have been accepted for generations. Do not believe spread rumours. Do not believe just because it is written in scripture. Do not believe because of the authority of teachers or elder people. But when you realise, that something is beneficial and that it helps the individual and everybody, then accept it and live by it."

What Is a Myth?

"Myths are stories of gods", wrote the philologist Jan de Vries [Vri61]. This is correct but by no means encompasses the full range of mythology, as Rudolf Simek remarked in his lexicon on Germanic mythology [Sim06b]. Often "only" demigods, other mythological creatures from the so-called "lower mythology", heroes and ordinary people appear in myths as well.

Nowadays myths are usually equated with fairy tales, an assessment which is fundamentally flawed in (mainly primary) religions, which have a rich choice of myths with great importance in religious practice. That assessment is based on the Christian belief structure in my opinion.

Christians who take the whole Bible literally see it completely as factual historic account. Of course many Christians do not take any Bible passage literally but recognize quite a lot as myth, especially in the Old Testament, e.g. the creation and the global flood. It is a bit different regarding the New Testament, especially the Gospels. The biography of Jesus and his resurrection in particular are mostly considered history. Confronting the historicity of religious texts with myths people have composed produces the notion that myths were just fairy tales and thus not suitable as a basis for a serious religion or as supportive teachings.

Actually the Old Testament contains very little real history. The Egyptologist Jan Assmann considers the exodus of the Israelites from Egypt to be totally legendary and beholds it as a cultural myth, which describes the transformation of Judaism from polytheism to monotheism [Ass03]. The same applies to the biblical conquest of Canaan. According to Assmann, it describes the above mentioned transformation too; historically the Israelites already lived in Canaan when the conversion took place. This is supported by the current research of Israeli and US-American archaeologists, who found no archaeological evidence for the exodus and the conquest, as well as some other Old Testament events [Fin04]. In addition, the forty years migration of the Israelites points out by itself that this is a myth. Professional caravans master that range in a few weeks; an entire nation perhaps in a few months. The number 40 is a code throughout the Bible for prolonged periods of time, whose actual length is not exactly known, and for stories that are transparently purely mythological. It can be compared to the temptation of Jesus by Satan in the desert, which lasted exactly 40 days (Matt 4:1-11).

To me, the Gospels are pure myths too, the Acts of the Apostles a founding legend with many mythological elements. It cannot be ruled out that Jesus might have been a historical role model, but what is told about his life in the Gospels has nearly nothing to do with such a hypothetical model. I also think that it is very possible that a historic person resembling the Biblical Jesus has never lived.

The first indication is the fact that there are no extra-biblical mentions of Jesus himself whatsoever. Tacitus wrote that a "Chrestus" (a Greek slave name) was crucified by Pontius Pilate and about whom the "Chrestians" had a "pernicious superstition", but this is rather a description of the Christian faith rather than a historical note [Tac92]. Furthermore Tacitus even misspelled the name of Jesus and his followers; probably he did not know any of them personally, only by hearsay. The only extra-biblical mention of Jesus, which indicates an actual historicity, comes from the Jewish historian Flavius Josephus and shows such a strong Christian influence that it is usually regarded as a later Christian addition to the original text [Jos11].

Another point is the obvious mythological aspects in the life of Jesus. Apart from all the supernatural actions such as walking on water, transformations of food and other miracles, the curriculum vitae of Jesus follows a typical mythological pattern. It starts with the birth in a cave. In ancient Palestine caves were utilised as stables, and the Church of the Nativity of Jesus in Bethlehem has been built in the 2nd century over a cave. Now it is archetypical for a God to be born in a cave; Hermes was born in one [Ros90], as well as Mithras, whose birth is also called "birth of the rock" [Klo06].

FitzRoy Richard Somerset published under his peerage as Lord Raglan a collection of commonly occurring events in the life of mythological heroes [Rag03]. This so-called "Lord Raglan scale" comprises 22 points, including birth by a royal virgin, being the son of a God, the attempt to kill him as a small child and mysterious circumstances around his death. A CV reaching more than six points on the scale is considered mythological, the hero considered a mythological archetype . He has not dared though to analyse Jesus in his book in that manner, but depending on the interpretation of some points in the list the Jesus of the Gospels scores between 15 and 19 points.

Its scale is very interesting but Lord Raglan's book also contains some errors. He treated the discovery of America by the Vikings as a myth, because at the time of the first edition's publication in 1936 there was no archaeological evidence yet. Meanwhile, even genetic markers have been found in the genome of Icelanders proving that some Native American ancestors were brought from America to Iceland [Sig10].

The attempt of Herod to kill Jesus right after his birth by murdering all newborn babies is mentioned nowhere else except the Bible, and it is extremely unlikely that the ruling Romans would have allowed a vassal king to do something like this and then have omitted to mention it somewhere. This episode only constructs Jesus' flight to Egypt as a fulfilment of an Old Testament prophecy about the future Jewish Messiah, namely related to the phrase "I called my son out of Egypt" (Hos 11:1).

I think it is quite likely that the story of Jesus is pure myth and not based on historical fact or that the life story of a historical Jesus was transfigured into myth including an apotheosis[4]. Keep in mind, I intend no pejorative statement here; myths obtain an outstanding importance on religious and ethical teachings.

What are myths about then? They contain poetic descriptions of natural events that are important to mankind, philosophical, ethical and moral teachings or religious justifications of historical circumstances. They contain ideas of mankind and the intercourse between humans and towards nature. Even if they were purely fictional, they reflect cultural backgrounds which are significant for the theory and practice of the connected religion.

I would like to give and explain three examples: the myth of Persephone [Gem86], the one of Thjalfi und Röskva [Sno91] and

---

[4] see page 50

The Song of the Nibelungs (*Nibelungenlied*) [Boo03]. Although the latter is a medieval legend referring to knightly love, it is based in part on pagan myths such as the Song of Sigurd or Sigfrid [Jor01], who is later called "Siegfried" in the Song of the Nibelungs. Furthermore it is interesting to look at them in relation to German history.

Persephone is the daughter of Zeus and Demeter, the Goddess of Fertility, who is also responsible for the growth and prosperity of grain, cereals (deriving from Ceres, the Roman name of the Greek Demeter), and other seeds. Hades wants to marry her and makes a marriage proposal to Zeus, who neither approves nor rejects it, because he knows that she would not voluntarily live in the sunless underworld. Hades takes the silence as consent and abducts her into the underworld, where she yields to her fate. But now Demeter is desperate and prevents the growth of all plants, which, in turn, brings Zeus to intervene. He procures an agreement that Persephone may now change her home in a half-yearly rhythm between the underworld and at the side of her mother.

This is clearly neither a historical report nor a cute fairy tale. Here is portrayed in a beautiful way, how the seasons, especially summer and winter, and the connected natural growth alternate. A somewhat naive believer may see this story as the reason, *why* there actually are summer and winter in the sense of a divinely given natural law, but thanks to simplest astronomical knowledge we should be beyond such a notion today. I think the ancient Greeks were already beyond that as well, at least the educated ones.

Some of the readers may know the legend of Thjalfi and Röskva from the Danish cartoon "Valhalla", which is based on a comic by Peter Madsen and relates the myth in a child-friendly form. On a trip, the two Gods Thor and Loki make a stop at a farmer's house. The farmer has two children, a son named Thjalfi and a daughter named Röskva. The Gods stay overnight, and Thor slaughters the goats that pull his wagon to eat them with Loki and the peasant family, however, he prohibits stirring their bones. The children do not comply, break one of the leg bones, and feast on the bone marrow.

The next morning, Thor brings the goats back to life and notices that one of them is lame because of the injured bone. This makes him pretty angry, because in the mythology the goats are involved in the process of creating thunderstorms. Their clop produces the thunder, and thus, the children's misbehaviour has global consequences (so to speak). Now, his reaction and punishment for this misconduct are interesting. He neither curses or disciplines them or their potential offspring nor simply forgives them, like some other God might do. Instead he takes them into his service and lets them work for him to pay off the damage they had caused.

I think this story teaches a moral lesson, namely how to punish misdeeds, neither excessively nor hardly at all. The damage should be undone if possible, by correcting or paying for it, and an additional punishment be applied to the persons responsible adapted to the gravity of the situation in order to prohibit crimes from appearing to be easy or even result in positive opportunities for those committing the crime. Thor expects certain behaviour for very important reasons, and his reaction to the disobedience shows how the society should deal with crimes or other offences. That may sound farfetched, but considerations like these show how to get useful teachings from mythological stories without treating them as historical events.

The Song of the Nibelungs is partially based on historical events such as the invasion of the Huns in the Migration Period. It was also assumed that the dragon slayer Siegfried represents the Cherusci Arminius defeating the three legions of Varus in 9 A.D., while the dragon depicts that Roman army [Höf61]. As the story should be well known, I will omit a summary of the entire content. Instead, I will concentrate on archetypical characteristics of the protagonists and their unyielding loyalty which became a phrase in the German language and culture, the so-called *Nibelungentreue* (*Treue* = "truth", "faithfulness", "loyalty"). Both fit into the previously illustrated way of how myths can be interpreted, and the latter had a notable negative effect on German history. In my opinion, this was due to a Christian interpretation of the archetypes instead of a pagan one, and the subsequent impact on allegiances and hierarchical structures in human societies.

Also beautifully depicted in the various film adaptations of the saga is Siegfried as the good and characterful hero, Hagen von Tronje as the sinister evil guy and king Gunther, as the intellectually and physically less equipped, who needs the help of his heroic subordinates to reach his noble goals. Siegfried's role as a hero is clear regarding the slaying of the dragon, which is also told in older sources. In my opinion, it no longer applies in the later stages of the medieval legend. Hagen is the left-over pagan, thus evil by nature, and all his actions are crimes. The ruling king is unfortunately somewhat incapable, but his subordinates obey and help him as they can and must. That is the common picture so far.

I interpret the characters differently. Hagen is the tragic hero, the good guy in fact, Gunther the despotic evil selfishly seeking power and wealth, and Siegfried the intellectually less equipped, who is shamelessly exploited by the king to achieve the royal goals.

The storyline of Brünhild is crucial for this interpretation. She expected to be courted by Siegfried, what may express her love towards him, but then Gunther asked her to marry him. To qualify as a suitable husband, the candidate had to defeat her in a fighting game, a task Gunther was not capable of. Siegfried brought him to victory undetected using his magic hood, the cloak of invisibility. This alone was not really gentlemanlike towards Brünhild. She rightly suspected a fraud and repeated the fighting game on the wedding night. Gunther would have to confess that he is a cheater but Siegfried helps him again with the cloak of invisibility, strictly speaking together they rape Brünhild. Hagen wants to avenge this crime, but due to Siegfried's invulnerability except for a single point on his body (an exact duplicate of Achilles in the Iliad) he is unable to fight him only by the means of physical violence. The alleged deceitful murder with preceding intriguing inquiries is therefore rather a stratagem against an otherwise invincible opponent to redress a crime than a crime itself.

In contrast to Siegfried Hagen acts quite honourably in the former cultural context, i.e. here and in other story lines. He just makes one crucial error in the saga: He is loyal to a wrong, even tyrannical ruler. He is not alone in that manner – the other

Burgundians do the same. But he is the protagonist, who symbolises the error due to which the whole people perish at the end of the day.

This loyalty of the Burgundians towards their king is not a virtue here but a warning on the possible negative consequences, if the sworn virtue is not mutually provided, up-down or from one side to the other.

In the Christian context, the unconditional loyalty of subordinates to the one on top and the grace from the ruler towards those at the bottom is normal. This corresponds to the mythological hierarchy with a supreme god on top. In Heathenism, especially the Germanic, loyalty is a bilateral matter[5]. It must be returned, as well and especially by the ruler or the military leader – something Gunther never does. If the loyalty is broken from one side the other is no longer obliged to comply.

In the German history there are some drastic examples of how the incorrect handling of loyalty ended in disasters. Whenever German rulers of the 19th or 20th century literally told the people to behold the *Nibelungentreue* as a virtue to follow, they led the country into a devastating war and ultimately into downfall and destruction. For the members of the military resistance movement in the 3rd Reich the oath of allegiance to Adolf Hitler personally was a serious obstacle in their effort to actively fight against him. His personal oath inhibited Stauffenberg for example for a long time to change his attitude to act as an assassin and kill the dictator to change the political system [Hof07].

This change would have come much sooner with a different and more pagan understanding of loyalty (see also page 126). An example is provided by Arminius, who is suspected to be the historical role model for Siegfried. He had been selected by several Germanic tribes to command their combined forces against the Romans; this role had expired after his victory. But he afterwards tried to establish himself as a king, maybe by using military force, whereupon he was liquidated by his own kindred. Now by modern understanding of law such a pre-emptive strike against a potential

---

[5] Mutual instead of one-sided giving and taking is also an aspect of pagan sacrifice practice, see chapter WHAT IS A SACRIFICE?

dictator may not be correct. The actual killing of an actual tyrant is still appreciated. Hardly anyone condemns Stauffenberg's assassination attempt as an evil crime, and in ancient times without a real rule of law provided by the government or a government at all there was nearly no other option for reasonably free people to get rid of an upcoming and unwanted dictator, especially if he could rely on armed forces.

Creation stories are a special kind of myth. Again, it is not advisable to see them as historical or scientific reports. Anyway, there is a significant difference between various creation myths told in various religions. There are those, as in Christianity, in which an eternal God creates the whole cosmos, and those, in which the cosmos emerges more or less on its own while the worshipped Gods came into existence within the cosmos somewhat later. The latter happens in Germanic and Greek myths.

A myth of the creation or of the structure of the universe is closely related to the cosmology or cosmological assumptions, no matter whether it is the creation by higher beings, a spontaneous occurrence, or eternal existence, perhaps in the form of cyclic periods. That is still philosophy and not science. But it is very close to science, thus comparisons to scientific cosmology can easily be made.

At the beginning, in the Germanic mythology, there is only the *Ginnunga-gap*, the "yawning gap". Out of nowhere appear two worlds, the world of fire (*Muspellsheim*) and the world of ice (*Niflheim*). The fire melts the ice, and the ice evaporates into the void and builds up the cosmos in the form of the giant Ymir [Poe12].

In Greek mythology the beginning is very similar. At first there is the *Chaos*, a totally disordered state. Then the cosmos arises in the form of the Titans, the most important is Gaia, the "Mother Earth" [Hes99].

In both cases, the Gods appear a few generations later and descend from different higher beings, the Giants (*Jotuns*) or Titans. The revered Gods are thus not really the creators of the whole universe. Please note that the assumption of other world or universes like an afterlife or the Nine Worlds are an exception here.

The worlds additional to the world of men or the universe inhabited by us belong as much to the whole cosmos as ours does.

Compared to one or several eternal gods creating the cosmos out of nothing, the other type of creation myths have two advantages in my opinion. Furthermore, they do imply a substantial difference about the nature of the involved gods.

The first advantage is the compliance with the current scientific knowledge. Although a myth should not be scientifically analysed in detail, a matching motive like a spontaneously occurring or self-creating cosmos is compelling. The cosmos' spontaneous appearance out of nothing is a widely accepted physical theory [Gut99]. I think a myth matching that theory is better than a non-matching one.

The interplay of fire, ice and empty space in the Nordic-Germanic creation myth can be seen as a poetic picture of the early expanding universe, when radiation and matter were separated because of the ubiquitous cooling caused by the expansion and which built up the current cosmological structure including galaxy clusters and background radiation [Wei77]. Muspellsheim, Niflheim and Ginnunga-gap form Ymir and Audhumbla, which can be interpreted as the cosmos' material structure in this context, in a very similar way. Before the Gods create the world of men, they kill Ymir to gain the material for the world from his remains. Physically the heaviest element that can be produced in stars by nuclear fusion is iron. Copper, silver, gold and iodine necessary for the human thyroid only exist because early generations of stars exploded as supernovae, whereby the elements heavier than iron were produced, which nowadays are necessary to build up the Earth and the life upon it. In other words, like the death of Ymir had to precede the human world, the death of stars in the physical universe had to occur before a planet suitable for men and life in general could exist.

This neither means nor indicates that our ancestors, who wrote down that myth, had recognised those physical circumstances or foresaw the modern astronomical findings. It just appears that they had cosmic ideas that match scientific knowledge far better than those of some religious competitors. Furthermore, I find it very interesting, what opportunities you have to interpret such a myth from a modern perspective, although this is not really necessary.

The second advantage is that an eternal god, who creates a finite universe, causes serious intellectual and even logical problems. To explain we must first define what "eternal" means. In this context there are two possible definitions, first an "infinitely long period of time", second "timeless".

Current cosmology assumes that the space-time appeared together with the universe [Haw88]. Therefore time before the big bang could not have existed, which makes the assumption of an eternally long period of time physically meaningless. However, there are also hypotheses that indicate other cosmological conditions, so that a pure physical objection against that definition is not enough.

A god who had existed infinitely long and at a certain point in time decided to create the universe, raises the question, why he has waited forever before he created the cosmos and what made the actual date so special that he acted just then and not an eternally far away point in time before or after.

This problem was known long before Christianity. The Epicureans argued in the first century B.C. against the Platonic image of a god, which was also based on an eternal creator [Cic95]: "To you [...] I ask the question, why the builders of the world have suddenly emerged after they have slept for countless centuries. Because, even if there was no world, there was the time [...]; now why [...] was your forethought idle during this immense amount of time? Did it shy away from the arduousness? But a God feels none, and there also was none, since all forces of nature, sky, fire, earth and water obey the divine powers."

To assume a cosmos finite in time within an infinitely long period of time, whose lifetime is always almost zero compared to eternity and which was intentionally created by entities living in that eternity, makes little to no sense.

To equate eternity with timelessness causes the above mentioned physical problem to disappear, but it produces some new ones. A timeless state cannot change. For a change it always takes time. If at one point in time t_1 a certain and specific state exists, it needs a different point t_2 so that a different state can exist. A timeless being, whether a god or not, could neither think nor plan, and thus cannot create a cosmos, because every action produces a change and that requires time. The only (auxiliary) verb, that does not require time, is “to be”. A timeless god could be but not act.

Furthermore if there was an eternal life after death, this life would also be timeless, i.e. without any possibility of change. A state of being, in which you cannot change, cannot act and cannot experience anything, cannot be called “life”. It does not differ from a final death without an afterlife.

These intellectual and logical difficulties explain why theologians, who take their God for a timeless being, allow for divine interventions in the world from real time to time. In my opinion, this causes even worse problems than anything else. How should that work physically, to have some real time from time to time to act in a state of total timelessness? That makes no sense at all.

The assumption that a creator of the cosmos is needed is based on a philosophical point of view, e.g. formulated by Titus Lucretius Carus [Car12]: *De nihilo quoniam fieri nihil posse videmus.* = “And we see, that nothing can derive from nothing.”, which is often shortened to *Ex nihilo nihil fit.* = “Nothing comes from nothing”.

It is presumed that everything that exists and especially everything, that did not exist forever, must have a cause. Thus the cosmos, which has a beginning, must have a cause that is identified with a previous or eternally existing god. Against this view there is a logical and a physical-philosophical objection, though the latter first occurred in the early 20th century.

The assumption of an uninterrupted cause-and-effect chain, which requires a cause for the cosmos, also requires that the existence of a creator has a cause. That produces an infinite regress, which is arbitrarily and without any logical reason stopped at one point, namely, at the existence of the divine creator. A “meta-god” creating the universe creating god could be declared as well, and thus the regress would be broken at that point. Or the chain of cause-and-effect is broken at the origin of the cosmos itself, making the philosophical necessity of a divine creator obsolete.

The Nobel Prize winners Niels Bohr and Werner Heisenberg formulated the so-called Copenhagen interpretation of quantum mechanics, which is now accepted by most physicists. It states that in the microscopic world indeterministic incidents permanently happen and a stable and for all effect applicable cause-and-effect chain does not exist. [Hei55]. This also applies to the origin of the universe, which can be regarded as a causeless quantum event. Due to the expansion of the universe its size at the beginning was in the subatomic range. At such small distances of space and time almost everything is energetically possible because of Heisenberg's Uncertainty principle [Hei27], even the emergence of a gigantic universe.

The dimensions of our universe pose another problem with deities who created the cosmos for the sake of mankind. Our world is only an incredible tiny part of it, there are probably countless more, on which life and probably also intelligence has evolved. To create such a gigantic structure only for the purpose of the human race makes little sense. That circumstance was not recognised at the time, in which the view of the world was limited due to the restrictive observation possibilities on the solar system and the sphere of fixed stars. Of course a divine creator may have intended far more with the cosmos than what is accessible or even revealed to us, but that does not sound very reasonable to me.

A hybrid between a divine creator and immanent polytheism is shown in two Egyptian creation myths, those from Memphis and the Ennead of Heliopolis [Sha91]. Here the God, who creates the entire cosmos including all other Gods, emerges from the Nun, the primordial sea, at first. In the myth of Memphis this is Ptah, the "builder master", and in the Ennead it is Atum, the "complete one" or creator of himself. The Nun can be compared to the Ginnunga-gap and the Chaos. The Tohu wa-bohu in the Old Testament is also very similar to them.

The disordered, waste and void state in scripture, whether it is called Ginnunga-gap, Chaos, Nun, or Tohu wa-bohu, is directly comparable to the cosmological state at the big bang as well, whether it was a nothingness or according to some newer theories a kind of quantum foam from which material universes emerge [Vil07]. Often there are additions in the myths indicating a cyclical emerging and decay of the cosmos, e.g. the appearance of a new world after Ragnarok in the Nordic myths. Such cycles also appear in modern cosmology. If the entire mass of the universe is large enough, such a cycle is inevitable [Wei77].

The empirical fact, that the universe expands and therefore must have had a beginning instead of existing eternally, is often regarded as a proof for a divine creation by religions which postulate such a creation. Interestingly, it was a Roman Catholic priest and astrophysicist Georges Lemaître, who formulated the first big bang theory [Lem27]. Overall there were only two seemingly available options: either a world with a beginning initiated by a transcendent creator or an eternal universe. Heraclitus already said [Stä06]: "This world [...] was neither created by a God nor by a human, but it was always, is always and will be always an eternal and living fire."

But the recent scientific findings allow both a cyclical and a finite cosmos spontaneously formed without a transcendent cause from a timeless nothingness or from a quantum foam, if the standard Copenhagen interpretation of quantum mechanics is philosophically accepted.

Considering all these circumstances I behold those myths, in which the cosmos appears before the Gods, as far better and much more compliant to scientific facts than those, in which the cosmos is created by one or several higher beings.

The myths that tell of the origin of mankind are also closely linked to scientific knowledge. The Gods are somehow involved in that process in all myths I know of, so one can ask how it fits with the biological theory of evolution, according to which life in general and therefore also the human race emerged and developed itself without planning or external influence.

Two things are important here. First, the already discussed case, that a myth contains a teaching which probably has nothing to do with anything describable by science, and secondly the conceptions applied to the Gods acting in the myths, which are discussed in detail in the next chapter.

If the gods are regarded as personified natural forces, as Jordan calls them *Ordner* (= "organisers", "guards") several times in his German translation of the Edda [Jor01], then the "creation" of man by those gods is a completely natural process.

Concerning the creation of man in the Völuspá, there are especially manifold ways of interpretation. Literally the Gods Odin, Hönir and Lodur find two tree trunks on the beach, which they transform into the first human couple named Ask and Embla (= "ash and elm") through the gift of various skills and abilities.

Now, the creation of man from trees is a very archaic myth [Tho58], and this picture may have been literally chosen by the narrators of the Völuspá, but other interpretations are possible.

The names of the people resembling trees may be purely symbolic or poetical, and the act of creation symbolises the first encounter of the Gods by man by receiving a set of certain skills from them. It is not about the biological creation of man but his cultural development towards civilization. The contact with the Gods, where the people receive gifts, which we can interpret as obtaining new types of knowledge, brings mankind on a new and higher stage of cultural development. Of course, evolutionarily this did not happen at a single point in time but over a very long period, a myth however can focus on a single literary event.

From today's perspective, we know of course that all living things on Earth are evolutionarily related, so that a modern interpretation of this story in the Völuspá can treat the picture of the trees as the biological relationship of man with all life forms including plants. That the Gods do not simply construct humans out of inanimate matter but "only" find them fits into this interpretation as well. I deliberately used the quotes, as "only" is not meant depreciatively, quite the opposite.

The similarities between myths from different times and cultures are interesting as well. As far as I can see, all Indo-European religions contain for example the struggle of a God, usually a weather-god, or hero against a serpent or a dragon. In the Vedas there is Indra against Vṛtrá [Thi77], the Hittites have Tarhun against Illuyanka [Sch65], the Greek Heracles against Hydra [Sch82], the Germans Thor against Jormungand, the Midgard Serpent, or Sigurd against the dragon Fafnir [Sim76]. In Christianity Satan is depicted as a serpent successfully fought by Jesus, and there is the legend of Saint George fighting a dragon [Vor07]. The struggle of a god or hero against a power that is threatening mankind is told in many different cultures over a long period of time in very similar images, which is not surprising as the myths contain archetypes which are of course identical even across cultural differences.

It is also interesting and amazing, how much of the ancient myths are reflected in common traditions and are practised by common folk, often without any knowledge of the mythological origin or relation to the old religions. In Germany there is the custom not to wash or hang laundry during the Christmas season. This is not a Christian work ban but probably goes back to the fear that the spirits of the dead, riding around at that time in Wodan's Wild Hunt, could get caught in a clothesline or the laundry and even steal it and it reuse during the following year as a shroud for the former owner. For more on the Twelve Days (*Rauhnächte*), when the Wild Hunt rages, see [Frü99].

Whether you agree with the contents of the myths or not, their cultural influence, how inconspicuous they might be, shows how much they reflect the human mind and basic views referred to in archetypical images.

It becomes complicated when myth is transmitted from one culture into the next, from one era to the next, and from one language into another. We know from discussions about Bible translations, that we often had to understand Greek or Hebrew to fully understand the content and the underlying intention. The same problem arises with the Nordic-Germanic myths written down in the Eddas in Old Norse, especially if the translation should also use a stave rhyme. This makes it very difficult to find a term matching to the original, and sometimes the translated result is totally confusing to the reader.

An example is from the Völuspá. It unfortunately makes little sense in the English translation of this book as the German Edda translations produce the above mentioned problems. I therefore have always cited the original German verses and translated them literally into English in order to illustrate those problems. I do not understand Old Norse or the still very similar Icelandic, yet I will write down the original verse in question [Mun47]:

Áðr Burs synir bjöðum um ypðu,
þeir er Miðgarð mœran skópu;
sól skein sunnan á salar steina,
þá var grund gróin grœnum lauki.

Simrock translated [Sim76]:

Bis Börs Söhne die Bälle erhuben,
Sie, die das mächtige Midgard schufen.
Die Sonne von Süden schien auf die Felsen
Und dem Grund entgrünte grüner Lauch.

(Until Bör's sons raised the balls,
They, who created mighty Midgard,
The sun in the south shone on the rocks,
And green leek grew on the ground.)

And Jordan did [Jor01]:

Bis Burs erzeugte die Zirkelbahnen
Geschaffen für sie, Worauf sie den schönen
Garten der Mitte gemodelt, die Erde.
Von Süden besonnt Ward die starre Steinflut
Und die Gründe grünten Von Gräsern und Kraut.

(Until Burs created the cyclic tracks,
Created for her, On whom they modelled
A beautiful garden in the centre, the Earth.
From the south illuminated, Was the stiff spate of stones
Grass and herbs were growing on the grounds.)

Balls? Cyclic tracks? The Google translator [Goo12] produces roughly "until Bur's sons lifted the burden" from the first line. But it does not know Old Norse, only Icelandic, which may result in the shift of meaning of various words. Combining Simrock's and Jordan's translations, we can interpret "balls" as planets and "cyclic tracks" as their orbits around the sun. I doubt this was really meant a thousand years ago, but the idea that the Gods not only arranged the Earth but the whole solar system is certainly not wrong.

Now, Henry Adams Bellows translated [Poe12]:

Then Bur's sons lifted the level land,
Mithgarth the mighty there they made;
The sun from the south warmed the stones of earth,
And green was the ground with growing leeks.

As it sounds prettier and is far closer to the original than the German attempts, I am taking this English translation as an example and am trying my own version:

Bald erhoben Burs Söhne das ebene Land
Das mächtige Midgard machten sie dort
Die Sonne im Süden schien auf die steinige Erde
Und grünes Gras wuchs auf warmem Grund.

WHAT IS A GOD?

This question raises the same problem as before regarding religion and faith. Most people only know the conception of God they have learned in school, or the teachings of their religion, and apply them to all Gods of all religions. In these parts it is the Christian notion, which can easily be applied to Judaism or Islam as well, but it fails at more alien religions, as we have already seen with Shintoism. This notion does not fit at all to its *kami*.

In this chapter we focus on the differences between what is called "God" in the Western world and the ideas about the Gods occurring in European Paganisms. In Heathenism those ideas are usually not dogmatic, but even people with different ideas about what a god actually is can follow the same religion and celebrate the corresponding rites using well known god-images from the myths.

The most important difference is between the *transcendence* of the Christian God and the *immanence* of the pagan Gods.

Transcendent means the world exceeding, otherworldly, or supernaturally – in any case by empirical experiences not fully determinable [Eis04]. A transcendent god is not part of this cosmos; he is eternal and based outside of it, but capable of intervening in this world. An immanent god, however, is part of the cosmos. Often regarded as immortal, which has little to do with the above mentioned concept of eternity, but also frequently viewed as being mortal like in the Germanic myths. This is directly related to the different types of creation myths. One type of myth with a creator and the other in which the universe arises spontaneously (see former chapter). Transcendent gods are or may be creators; immanent ones arise later in the existing cosmos and then control its development and evolution or bring order to its chaotic conditions.

The pagan Gods are mostly considered immanent because in the pagan Greek and Germanic myths the Gods are born several generations after the creation of the cosmos, although there may be heathens who have a transcendent image of them. The idea of transcendence came up in ancient times – Plato was an outstanding advocate – so that it could have been adopted even by pre-Christian cults. But if you take a closer look at many circumstances the Gods experience in the myths, e.g. Balder's death or Hephaestus' limping or the interwoven family relationships, then immanence is a more appropriate alternative for the pagan Gods, if you ask me.

Another topic that supports the immanence of the Gods is the often encountered *apotheosis*, the deification of an ordinary human, usually after his death. Such a God is naturally a part of the cosmos. One example is found in the Roman emperor cult; but only very rarely a still living emperor was worshipped. Pliny the Younger wrote about the living Emperor Trajan [Kla96]: "Let us never flatter him like a God, like a higher being – because we are talking not of a tyrant, but of a citizen, not of a lord, but of our father." The postmortem apotheosis, however, was accepted.

Another example can be found in Germanic Heathenism with Bragi, the God of poetry. This God does not appear in writing until very late in the 12th century and is most likely an apotheosis of the scald Bragi Boddason, who lived and composed in the 9th century [Sim06a]. Also the Egyptian scholar and architect Imhotep, the probable architect of the first pyramid was later worshipped as a God [Wil77].

If Jesus had a historical role model, we can even talk apotheosis here. Without wanting to dive into Trinitarian theology at the moment, this man was raised to a God or to one person of a triune God. Christians of course have a different view on this topic, for them this person[6] is an eternal part of an eternal God. This person was a human for a limited period of time. From a religious studies point of view, I see no difference in the historical process to other apotheoses.

The terms "god", *Gott*, or *gud* and *guð* in the Scandinavian languages, and *deus* or *theos* (θεός) respectively have an interesting etymology.

The northern European variants probably derive from the Indo-Germanic **gheu-* = "to pour" or **ĝhau-* = "to invoke", *theos* from

[6] In Christian theology the meaning of the term "person" is not the modern one. *Persona* here means "mask of an actor", thus the Trinity does not have the polytheistic approach as many suspect [Boe47].

thyein (θύειν) = "to sacrifice (by a burnt offering)" [Gri12]. Therefore we can conclude that "god" originally meant an entity to whom sacrifices are offered, as in the case of the pouring a libation. This fits to the pagan practice of sacrificing (see chapter WHAT IS A SACRIFICE?).

Deus may simply be the Latin variant of *theos* but may also have an older Indo-Germanic heritage and derive from **djew-* = "heaven" or "sky" [Sch23]. From **djeus ph2tēr* = "Heavenly Father" came Zeus Pater (Ζεῦς πάτερ) and in Latin Jupiter (*Iuppiter*, from *Iovius pater* and *Diēspiter*) [Sch23]. There are connections to the ancient Indian *deva* (देव) = "heavenly entities" or "the luminous" and the Vedic *Dyauṣ Pitā* (द्यौष् पिता), which also means "Heavenly Father" and is mentioned in the Rig-Veda [Obe98].

In the Indo-Germanic language the personified heaven is called **deiwos-*, from which the name of the ancient Germanic God Tiwaz or Teiwaz is derived, that later changed to Ziu, Zio and Tyr. Tyr appears as a pure God of War in the Poetic Edda, which might be related to the common identification as Mars in the *interpretatio Romana*. From his name's etymology he has a close relationship to Zeus and can therefore be seen as a Heavenly Father as well.

The Heavenly Father is most often accompanied by Mother Earth. In the Rig-Veda we have the above mentioned *Dyauṣ Pitā* and *Pṛthivī Mātā* (पृथिवी माता), in Semitic religions Baal and Astarte. "Baal" means "lord" or more generally "God" and was in ancient times commonly used as the name of the local supreme God [Ste01]. Astarte equals Ashtoreth or Ishtar and is mentioned in the Bible, where she is adored by king Salomon (1 Kgs 11:5). An ancestral link between Baal and Yahweh is likely, even though in the Old Testament Baal is a symbol for false idols and will be regarded as a demon or devil in later Christianity. Thus the devil's name Beelzebub derived from Baal Zebub = "Lord of the Flies" (Βααλ μυῖαν in the Septuagint), was in turn is a parody of Baal Zebul = "Exalted Lord". The Vulgate still says Beelzebub, the German translation Luther-1984 Baal-Sebub, and the current

Einheitsübersetzung[7], finally matching the original, Beelzebul (2 Kgs 1:3). Interestingly, all English Bible versions I checked (NIV, TNIV, NIRV, KJV, ESV, NASB, RSV, ASV, YLT, DBY) print Baal-Zebub except for some hyphens and apostrophes.

Astarte was also identified with Hera, the wife of Zeus [Bud04]. Hera (Ἥρα) is the feminine form of *heros* = "Lord". However, in the Greek myths the aspect of the Earth Mother and Goddess of Birth passed to Demeter and Eileithyia, Demeter as a sister and Eileithyia as the daughter of Zeus and Hera [Hes99].

In my opinion, to symbolize the sky as a man and the earth as a woman has a simple reason, namely the sexual component of rain falling from the sky on the earth as an image of fertilisation. The ruling couple before Zeus and Hera was Uranus and Gaia with a far deeper symbolic aspect of heaven and earth. It is Uranus' semen, according to Hesiod his blood that fell on Gaia, the Earth, and begat the giants, the Erinyes (Goddesses of Vengeance) and the Meliae (nymphs of the ash tree).

Now there are far more views on immanent gods than most monotheistic educated people normally could guess.

The real and slightly higher entity, seen as some kind of spirit, is a notion which comes closest to the monotheistic concept. Thus most people think it is the one adopted in Paganism as well. Depending on the detailed views of the follower, those entities are roughly similar or identical to the mythical god-images. This, in my opinion, quite naïve concept is widely followed though, but the religious reality is not that simple. Only a few have such a verbatim interpretation of the mythical descriptions. Most combine them with conceptions described below or do not recognise them at all. That does not only apply to modern Pagans but was also practised in the antiquity. Even Epicurus, who by the way was no atheist but told his disciples to worship the Gods, did say [Kla96]: "So in fact, there are Gods, to recognise them is immediately obvious. But they are not of the kind the masses imagine them. [...] Without God is not the one

---

[7] a modern standard translation done by Catholic theologians with the participation of the Protestants

neglecting those images but who follows those conceptions." Now this passage is easy to misunderstand, I think it states that the images described in the myths do not or do not completely correspond to reality and that the Gods are far more or there is something else behind those images.

Another idea is that polytheistic gods are incarnations of a single higher god. This can also be found in Hinduism and Stoic philosophy. The sole supreme god is not a person like in monotheism but rather a cosmic principle, which the Stoics called Logos and is often translated as "word" but should be better translated as "sense" or "reason". The Logos is the inherent and omnipresent principle in the universe that maintains and keeps it running orderly. Nowadays it could be seen as the entirety of natural laws. Then the gods as incarnations of that principle represent individual aspects of the cosmic order.

Close to that idea is the conception that gods are personified natural forces. Usually those forces of nature are good for the people, the gods as anthropomorphic images are well-meaning towards mankind. Gods of Fertility are an excellent example here. Negative forces are represented as Giants in the Norse and as Titans in Greek mythology, though not every Giant and Titan is an enemy of mankind (and thus of the Gods). We have to note that this conception is not an explanation for natural phenomena. We know today how weather activities like a tempest occur, gods throwing lightning bolts as not necessary as a scientific explanation but as a poetic image appropriate to honour the positive aspects of nature.

Very similar to that is to see the gods as personifications of cultural, civil, or other human concepts like values and ideals. Odin for example is a symbol of the quest for knowledge and wisdom then. This conception is by no means a new one. It can found in the teachings of Epicurus in which gods are ideals "the wise is following and trying to realise through philosophy" [Kla96].

Incidentally, these conceptions exist in a certain way independently from mankind, so that they can interact with people. The philosopher Karl Popper formulated this beautifully in his *Three-Worlds-Theory* [Pop78], even though I do not accept that the world 2 and 3 should have their own transcendent existence outside of world 1. This is very similar to Plato's world of ideas. World 1 is the real physical world, World 2 the individual human mind, and World 3 the overall collection of ideas, concepts, theories, etc. shared by some, many, or even all people. This World 3 is, due to the largely accepted concepts, an objective matter in equally large parts. Its contents have influence on the life of the individual human, even if they are purely mental constructs difficult to find in the material world. The human mind, World 2, is the interface between the real and material World 1 and World 3, the world of ideas.

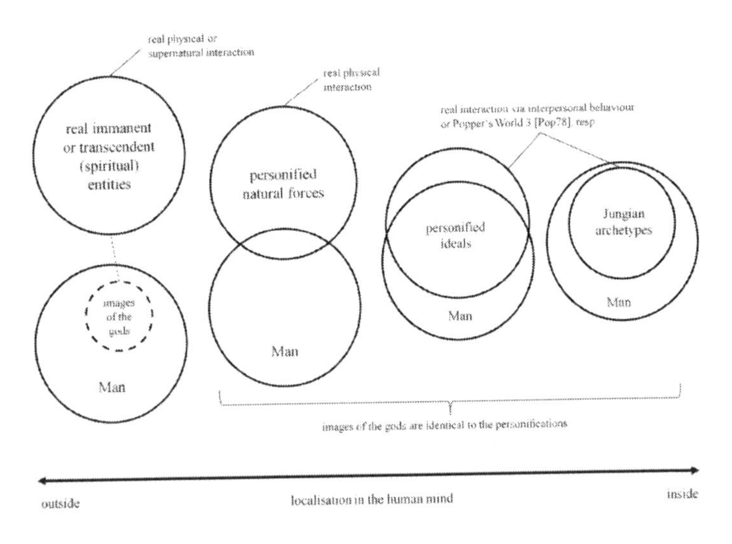

Figure 5: Basic pagan god-conceptions

As an example, I would like to state numbers, a construct that precisely and practically describes many things within nature and human civilization. The natural numbers can be understood as an abstraction of real, countable things occurring in nature, but that does not work for elements of other sets of numbers like negative, real, or complex numbers. As the old mathematician joke about negative numbers says, if four guys leave a room filled with three guys, one must enter again to have an empty room. Physically, this is of course utter nonsense, but nevertheless negative numbers describe a lot of things very well. And, to get a connection to normal life, negative numbers have an incredible strong and formative impact on people, as everybody knows who has too much of them on his account statement. This may sound funny but it illustrates how much influence those abstract concepts have on our lives. If those concepts are valuable or honourable ideals, we are moving into the field of religion. Anthropomorphic and personalised images of those conceptions can then be called "Gods" and worshipped.

Another god-conception is to treat a god as a Jungian archetype after the teaching of the psychologist Carl Gustav Jung [Jun01]. An archetype is a collective role model of human behaviour. To identify the gods with those archetypes or an idealistic view of them, means humans who worship them try to reach that ideal or live according to the archetypical role model. This is very similar to the above said personified ideals and concepts, it just concentrates more on the subconscious mind and a possible biological basis while the former conception is more about social and cultural ideas and interaction.

Although the idea of archetypes is rather present in modern Paganism (an earlier form and thus a similar view in ancient times probably did not exist), the personality of Jesus Christ is often interpreted as a "central and ultimate archetype" [Saa95].

The above said conceptions are often mixed and combined, in my experience only rarely will you find someone having only a single one of them. Personally I follow the conceptions of personalised natural forces and ideals. I behold Epicurus' teaching that the Gods are ideals you should follow for one of the wisest ever taught in history. In my opinion, this following does not need to be of a philosophical nature, there are many and not mutually exclusive alternatives, e.g. the ritual worship.

This view is purely naturalistic; it does not require any belief in the supernatural. The same applies to the psychological archetypes. It may sound surprising to many people that someone can follow a religion without assuming or accepting supernatural phenomena, but it does not contradict the definition of the term "religion" as made by Cicero and explained on page 16ff, which is not based on faith but on the adherence to traditions and rites.

A naturalistic god-conception also fits well to the myths in which the cosmos appears first and the Gods later. An immanent god is subject to the laws of the cosmos in which he was born, so that otherworldly, supernatural, or other unexplained properties are not really necessary. One may argue that such a conception is completely unnecessary and superfluous for the explanation of the cosmos, but such an explanation is exactly what a religion should be concerned with. Religion should rather be about the way how to live in this cosmos (see page 20), a question such immanent gods can answer very well if you ask me. The religious views are of a subjective nature and cannot be generalised or apply to all people.

In addition, there is no solid logical or empirical evidence against such a naturalistic concept. That any positive proof of the Gods' existence, cosmological, teleological, or ontological, does not work at all was already shown by Immanuel Kant who then constructed a moral proof [Kan81].

There are certain divine attributes though which can be disproved. Omnipotence and omniscience are the best examples. In their common meaning "is able to do anything" and "knows everything" they are mathematically impossible, as they directly lead to Russell's antinomies [Rus03]. An almighty could create a stone, he could not lift; the all-knowing would know how it felt not to know something. Russell formulated the paradox of a Barber being defined as someone who shaves all and only those who do not shave themselves [Rus18]. Is he able to shave himself? Both answers, yes or no, lead to a contradiction to the definition of the Barber, the question cannot be answered. Theologians then like to restrict the extent of omnipotence and omniscience to avoid running into those logical traps. But then those properties' distinguishing element towards other god-conceptions fails entirely.

In addition to the omnipotence and omniscience, the Christian God is also omnibenevolent leading to the so-called "theodicy-problem" [Lei10]. An omnipotent and omniscient creator, who loves all people, would not have created such an imperfect world filled with disease, tsunamis, earthquakes and other extremely deadly natural phenomena. With less powerful Gods living in conflict with other higher powers such as Giants and Titans, this is neither surprising nor a philosophical or logical problem.

Naturalistic and immanent gods are not perfect, but that just keeps them from the automatically occurring logical contradiction triggered by this alleged perfection. You can subjectively accept or reject them, but there is no objective argument for or against them. Regarding Paganism I have to repeat that it is not important to have faith in such a conception but to worship the Gods or their images displayed in the respective mythology. If that worship has a positive influence on an individual's personal life and its related lifestyle, even a partial or complete objective falsehood of such conceptions is nothing negative.

The conjoint worship of the same god-images with different god-conceptions behind them is and was common in Heathenism. This is not a modern practice, celebrating the same rituals together despite different notions about the Gods was everyday business in the ancient times [Cic95].

Bias of Priene, one of the so-called "Seven Sages of Greece" said already in the sixth century B.C. [Mar99]: "Speak of the Gods as they are." It does not matter here, *what* they are, in the sense of a detailed and objective factual description, you just accept, *that* they are, which enables a personal relationship with them and makes a ritual worship possible without almost automatically generating a potential dispute between members of the same religion but with different conceptions of the gods or different beliefs.

I can report from my very own experience, that the shared ritual worship of Gods does not necessarily require a unique religion or a unique god-conception of all participants. Often and even usually followers of different religions and befriended atheists do participate in our rituals. As long as everybody is complying to the few and easy to follow ritual rules, it is not a problem to invoke Gods from a different pantheon or none at all. Whenever an annual celebration is pending we invite all our friends and close relatives regardless of their religious views and memberships, and if they are present at the feast they are of course allowed to participate in the rites without being required to. Whoever wants to participate does so, who does not want to, does not.

To prefer friendly and familial relations over religious memberships and allegiances here has nothing to do with a missionary effort but is in fact a result of the following virtues, which are highly respected in Germanic Paganism: Trust, loyalty to friends and relatives, and hospitality toward those who were initially invited (about the virtues see also page 123).

For someone, whose religion does not demand the rejection of all the Gods of other religions, it is neither forbidden nor discouraged to worship or to pray to other Gods. For example, the geographical location of a rite has an influence on many heathens. To invoke Greek Gods when you are in Greece would be a pretty normal behaviour, even if you were no Hellenist.

The decision whether Gods of religions other than the ones of the gathered followers may be invoked in a ritual or not belongs to those who are gathered. Certainly there are many who do not allow that practice in their own rituals but who have no general problems with the Gods of other religions. They would even participate in the rites of those religions. Personally I do not mind. A ritual should give something to the participants, what God is involved is a decision of the practising ritualists and not of a dogmatically set liturgy.

Taking the above mentioned god-conceptions in mind, it can be seen that different god-images are just different perspectives of the same subject which they are representing. The natural forces, ideals, or archetypes are usually differently summarised and combined in the different pantheons. Thus Thor has attributes of Zeus and Heracles, Odin those of Hermes and, in my opinion, Apollon. The characteristics and "management functions" of the Gods of different religions are not always identical, but because these attributes do not need to be dogmatically believed, that does not pose any problems.

But even if you behold the Gods as real distinct entities, foreign Gods are nothing that you must reject or neglect. Either the other Gods are considered as additional entities or as different images of the same entities. The question, what image might be the true one, is not asked, as everybody knows that the images themselves are man-made pictures of something else.

The ancient Greeks had an altar, which was intended to serve the worship of all unknown Gods. They were aware of the fact that the own pantheon may not cover the whole extent of the divine.

Such an altar is described in the Acts of the Apostles, when Paul was visiting Athens (Acts 17:23ff). It is called "To the Unknown God", and that name has prevailed in Western literature due to the Biblical template. Due to that episode of the New Testament, the intention of this altar is, in general, greatly misconceived in Christianity. The so-called "unknown God" is viewed as a presentiment of the Christian God or a monotheistic god respectively, who covers all divinity including the parts the Greeks feared to have overlooked.

However, the ancient Greek historian Pausanias describes these altars explicitly using the plural [Spi03], [Paul8]: βωμοὶ δὲ θεῶν τε ὀνομαζομένων Ἀγνώστων = "Altars of the Gods called the Unknown".

In 1909 an altar was found in the sanctuary of Demeter in Pergamon, dated in the 2nd century and bearing the inscription: θεοις αγ[νωστοις] καπιτ[ων] δαδονχος = "Kapito the torch-bearer [consecrated this altar] to the unknown Gods" [Sch02].

I think it is clear that this altar was not intended to honour a yet unknown supreme and exclusive god, a gap that Paul wanted to fill with his God, but a variety of possibly so far unrecognised Gods. Possibly the author of the Acts of the Apostles also deliberately chose the mistaken singular to explain his own or the Christian view back then, so that the altar inscription "To the Unknown God" never really existed and only appears in the Bible and subsequent literature.

The Romans worshipped many foreign, i.e. non-Roman Gods: Mithras, Isis, Kybele, Attis, Serapis, and several more. The background might lie in the conquest and assimilation of many countries and peoples that kept to following their own religions. Their Gods were not included in the State religion, but were revered privately in clubs and mystery cults even by Roman citizens themselves.

It was customary for Germans in the Roman service to erect votive stones, even though they always used the Latin names of their Gods according to the *interpretatio Romana*, the Roman identification [Sim06a]. If a non-Roman deity is meant, it can be identified based on the names of the sponsors and epithets of the Gods. Examples are *Mercurius Cimbrianus* = "Mercury of the Cimbri", who is identified with Wodan/Odin, *Mars Thingsus*, often interpreted as Tyr/Ziu/Saxnot and *Hercules Magusanus*, whose epithet probably originates in the Germanic language (*mag-* = "to be able to") and who is identified as Donar/Thor. To honour the latter, even coins were minted in 261 A.D. [Sim06a]. In the Roman Empire he was portrayed exactly like Hercules though, with a lion's skin and a club, but the epithet and the sponsors' names of the corresponding stones clearly point to a Germanic God. Thus the Romans had money mentioning Thor.

Well, the identification of foreign Gods with one's own is not that simple, because the Gods' individual attributes are distributed differently over the pantheon. Tacitus wrote that the Germans worshipped Mercury and Hercules as their highest deities [Tac07], who were identified with Wodan/Odin and Donar/Thor. Looking at the way the Germans translated the Roman weekday names into their own, the interpretation Mercury = Wodan is confirmed as *dies Mercurii* = "Day of Mercury" and thus became Wodans' day = Wednesday. In the later Christian German Empire this name was transformed into *Mittwoch* = "middle of the week", however, in English it is still preserved. But Thor's day = Thursday falls on *dies Iovis* = "Day of Jupiter". Here, the Germans identified Jupiter with Thor instead of Hercules, probably due to the mutual throwing of lightning. The Roman identification with Hercules derives from his symbolism for strength and power, as Thor is indeed the strongest of all the Germanic Gods.

For the other days of the week you can also identify between Roman and Germanic deities, see the table below. The days of the moon and the sun were directly adopted. It is interesting that the gender of the involved Gods is exactly the other way around, corresponding to the grammatical gender. While in Romance languages Sol is masculine and Luna feminine, in German Sunna is feminine just like *die Sonne* = "the sun" and Mani like *der Mond* = "the moon" masculine. The name Friday comes from Odin's wife Frigg, in Old High German called Frîja. The southern Germanic name has prevailed in Scandinavia, Frîadagr in Old Norse [Sim06b]. Frigg is often identified with Hera/Juno, while Aphrodite/Venus is rather an interpretation of Freya. I think the latter is more suitable than to identify Frigg as Venus, but the original translators of the weekday names obviously thought different about that.

Roman God	Weekday		German God
Luna	*dies Lunaris*	Monday	Mani
Mars	*dies Martis*	Tuesday	Ziu/Tyr
Merkur	*dies Mercurii*	Wednesday	Wodan/Odin
Jupiter	*dies Iovis*	Thursday	Donar/Thor
Venus	*dies Veneris*	Friday	Frîja/Frigg
Saturn	*dies Saturni*	Saturday	-
Sol	*dies Solis*	Sunday	Sunna

Table 1: Identification of Roman with German Gods by the names of the weekdays

Oddly enough, there is no Germanic God, on whom the name of *Samstag* = "Saturday" is based. *Samstag* is derived from the Sabbath [Sch05], meaning "day of rest". In Icelandic it is called *laugardagur* = "laundry day". Perhaps nobody wanted to assign the name of a God to a day of rest, maybe in the Germanic mythology no God was found to properly match Kronos/Saturn. As the God of Sowing, Saturn could be equated with Freyr, the God of Fertility. Kronos, leader of the Titans and defeated by Zeus, could be interpreted as Ymir slain by the Nordic Gods. Neither fits nor feels right.

Thus, a distinct and general equalisation of Gods from different pantheons is not always possible. But as there is usually no dogmatic statement of faith regarding a distinct and for all people liable pantheon in Paganism, it rarely leads to quarrels.

What Is Atheism?

This chapter is not supposed to give a detailed explanation of atheism or to be a counter-argument or denouncement. As long as no atheistic motivated ideology or politic wants to ban religions, just because they are religions, there is nothing which can be brought against the stance not to believe in any god, not to worship them, and/or not to follow any religion. It is part of religious freedom, an important basic and human right, which protects not only beliefs and religions other than the majority adheres to, but also the personal attitude not to have a faith or a religion.

The Roman Empire allowed its citizens to follow as many religions as they wanted, even though temporarily some of them were prohibited and their followers persecuted (but out of political not religious reasons or those connected to the official faith). This can be regarded as positive freedom of religion. However, everyone was forced to take part in the Roman State religion, so there was no negative freedom of religion with regard to this official one. When Christianity became the official State religion, it unfortunately had forgotten its own experiences with its persecution and did not introduce a general negative freedom of religion but abolished the positive one.

There have always been atheists, i.e. people who declare gods for non-existent [Cic95]. But today's Western atheism began as a counter-movement to Christianity, starting with the Age of Enlightenment and supported until today by many philosophers like Ludwig Feuerbach [Feu41]. Most of the atheist arguments against religion, faith and gods are aimed directly against Christianity. If they are not specifically tailored to details solely found in the Christian faith, then they apply against Judaism and Islam as well, since these religions are very similar to Christianity. In ignorance of other definitions of the term "religion" than the Christian one or of different god-conceptions other than the transcendent creator, and of the varying significance of faith in other religions, all religions are regarded equally and thus believed that an argument against the Abrahamitic monotheisms is an argument against any religion.

Also the recent, so-called "New Atheism" with its most famous protagonist, the evolution biologist Richard Dawkins [Daw07], is a reaction on efforts mostly undertaken by Evangelical fundamentalists to remove scientific knowledge about the earth's age and evolution from the school curriculum. Those evangelical efforts also propose to teach children in public schools that mythological events can be taken as historical reports and can be instead understood as alternative scientific theories. This ostensible scientific theory is called "Intelligent Design", but is in fact only a disguise for the biblical creation story. These efforts have increased in recent years and it is not surprising that representatives of the maligned science defend real science against those efforts.

The new atheists' arguments are mostly of a scientific nature and refute the events described in the myths as things that could have never happened due to physical or logical reasons. This procedure may be correct regarding a religion in which certain or even all parts of the mythology have to be believed in. It is useless against a religion whose followers behold their myths as something different from factual reports anyway (see chapter WHAT IS A MYTH?).

Scientific or logical arguments work only against factual statements and logical constructs and not against ethics, values and ritualistic acts. You may be against the latter, because you have different ideas about ethics, values and the way of and the attitude to life, but this is on nearly the same plane as voting for a different party in a parliamentary democracy, and you would rather not have scientific or mathematical justifications or evidence to support your political stance.

Such rebuttals may work against statements of individual faith and whole religions but not against religions in which a prescribed faith or dogmas do not appear, are not constituent, or not binding for their followers. Religions in terms of Cicero's definition (see page 16) are not susceptible to these types of arguments. Only the circumstance that Western atheists as most citizens of the Western world only know one form of religion and mistakenly take this as a pattern for all religions, leads to the notion that certain scientific statements or logical conclusions against one form of religion would automatically disproof any religion.

A further often misunderstood topic is agnosticism which is closely related to atheism and roughly means "teaching of the unknown" or "not knowable". Many people, mainly religious ones, think agnostics would have a little bit of faith in God or would be halfway convinced of his existence. Basically they would be halfway between an atheist and a believer.

Atheism is a factual statement regarding the gods, namely it either denies their existence or, to be more diplomatically expressed, does not believe in them as the case may be. Agnosticism, however, is an epistemological position.

Agnosticism neither claims to know whether there have ever been gods or not nor that there is a probability of 0.5 for and against their existence. It claims there would be no way to find a proof for the existence of the gods, neither scientific nor logical. Therefore there can be no empirical or philosophical reason to believe in or worship a god, and thus no one can make a dogmatic or objectively reasonable statement about them.

The border to atheism is indeed vague, but an agnostic can be both an atheist and a believer or a religious practitioner as the case may be. They just do not accept any proof of the gods' existence or other arguments for their existence, as those are impossible due to the epistemological basis of agnosticism or they must be nonetheless wrong or meaningless, even if formulated.

Furthermore they do not accept statements of faith or ostensibly historical events, if there is clear scientific evidence against them [Hux89]. This is very close to atheism and is why most agnostics are also atheists, so that both views are grouped together despite the different and incompatible categorisation.

The Greek philosopher Protagoras formulated the probably oldest traditional agnostic statement in the fifth century B.C. [Die07]: "Regarding the Gods, it is impossible to know whether they exist or not or what their shape is like. The forces preventing me from knowing are so numerous, and also the question is confusing and human life too short."

In my opinion, both atheist and agnostic positions can only be held regarding specific and defined god-conceptions. This is a point often overlooked owing to the notion that you might suppose there is only one or several very similar concepts of the gods.

Thus you can regard one god-conception to be impossible, i.e. being an atheist towards that kind of god, while you view some other notion as possible or meaningfully defined. If it is pleasing or admirable, there is nothing to speak against the practice of the religion in which this notion is present and accepted. Via a common and respected *god-image* one can have a commonly practised and followed religion, although one adherent may be an atheist regarding the *god-conception* in terms of the next follower of the very same religion.

Now, some may think that any god-conception was impossible, meaningless or unnecessary and thus be an atheist to any kind of god. To classify the naturalistic ideas of gods as a personalisation or Jungian archetypes, as in the previous chapter explained, as impossible or unnatural is obviously not correct. To consider them nonsense or needless for one's own life is a matter of your personal attitude towards life, which is not an objective case and to be respected of course.

If we move from god-conceptions to the Gods themselves, it can be seen that monotheists especially are atheists towards any other God apart from their own, i.e. if they do not deem them as demons or something similar, which is not a rejection of their existence but of their divine nature. Usually polytheists do not categorically deny the existence of other Gods than their own, they are, as already mentioned, interpreted as different images of the same divine entities or just regarded as additional Gods.

There is the impression that atheists fight religion in general, especially the "new atheists" who publish many books and are frequently seen on television and the internet. The impression is a little deceiving – just because someone does not wish to participate in any religion, it does not mean he wants to ban all religion or convert all religious people to atheists.

Their actions are rather directed against the political influence of the great religions attempting to regulate the life of every person, be it a member of those religions or not. And that is not intended to be against harmless proselytising but against regulations and laws that force certain behaviour onto everyone implied by the main or official religion in the State but without any social or rational need. This concerns not only atheists, but also members of other religions.

Furthermore religions, which allegedly contain the absolute truth in respect to values, ethics and morals, often accuse non-members and especially atheists as having no values, ethics and morals at all. Someone who does not have faith in anything, in a religious sense, could not possess anything like that, or they could only be granted by a specific god.

Of course, atheism taken as a statement of fact of a denial of the gods' existence does not provide any values or ethics either. That does not mean atheists cannot gain those from other sources. There are great numbers of non-religious traditions, views and ideologies, so that the above said insinuation is always abusive and provokes countermeasures. In principle, if the values of one religion are treated as absolute ones, it also affects members of other religions, not only atheists, with different values. They are not supposed to have a lack of ethics only a false set of them. Now you may regard certain values as right and others as wrong, however, as long as the lack of a value or the possession of one contrary to it does not yield any disadvantage to other people, e.g. the lack of the values to respect other people's life and health, we are within the boundaries of freedom of opinion and expression. To request religiously based values from everyone and force them into social norms, such as to prohibit homosexual marriage or gender-dependent clothing laws, is at a minimum an affront and more often a crime against atheists and followers of different faiths.

(The following paragraphs refer to the legal situation in Germany.)

According to the German constitution, there is no State Church in Germany (Art. 140, Art. 137 WRV – an article that has been adopted from the *Weimarer Reichsverfassung* = "Weimar Constitution"). Also, contrary to popular opinion, there is no State recognition of religions. Whoever wants to establish an association or other organization, which operates as a religion, can do so without conditions or restrictions. Special legal regulations only apply if the establishment is intended for a socially relevant business (or if the State claims it would do exactly that). E.g. when operating a cemetery the laws regarding burials, which are clearly dominated by the Christian burial culture, are applied. Although they do allow private cemeteries. A religious association may gain the status of a *Körperschaft des öffentlichen Rechts*, something like a public corporation, if it meets the several necessary conditions. If this has happened, the association may collect its member fees through the state tax office via so-called "church taxes". By the way, this is not an obligation but a right, which is rarely neglected though[8], and the state tax offices raise fees for the association to collect their payments.

The connections between the major Christian churches and the State are so numerous and profound that there is no practical difference to an existing official State cult and through this, the constitutionally guaranteed freedom of religion (Art. 4 (1), (2)) is severely damaged. Not debatable is that the churches want and are allowed to deliver a television program to their millions of members. Why they send representatives to the public television broadcasting councils, who determine the programme of all recipients, however, is. That a faithful Christian celebrates important rites on Good Friday is also not debatable. That all citizens are prohibited from hosting or visiting a public dance is pure insolence. That the burial and treatment of corpses is legally controlled is completely understandable due to hygienic concerns. A clear breach of freedom of religion is that the ashes of a deceased person, which is chemically inert and can cause no harm to the living, must be buried. In many religions, especially Asian ones, it is customary to keep the ashes in urns at home.

There are many such examples. They do not only concern atheists but also followers of other faiths and religions, and they inevitably lead to unnecessary problems and disputes. The solution is a secular or even a laicistic State, which keeps a careful and complete separation of State and religion. The State neither promotes nor impedes any religion. Of course, this does not exclude

[8] To my knowledge Jehovah's Witnesses do not raise church taxes.

a persecution of communities and individuals who commit crimes for religious reasons.

Even the followers of the major religions would benefit from such a State at the end of the day. The probability of the following example is very low in Germany, but quite high in the United States: There are Evangelical denominations that consider the Roman Catholic Church to be a satanic organisation [Dan06]. If you are a Catholic in Germany, this is noted on the tax deduction card. Therefore the tax office and the office for public order know about it, the human resources department in the company you work for knows about it, and maybe your boss knows about it as well. If you have a boss who belongs to such a denomination, you may face serious problems.

Although it is part of the Christian tradition to communicate and confess their faith and through that their church membership, even at utmost risk to everybody else, this does not apply to all religions. In a pluralist environment, it is part of personal freedom to be allowed to withhold information regarding your faith, your religion and your attitudes from your manager, your company, the State, or anyone else. The best example for that freedom is the democratic election. Your vote is secret to protect your free political disposition. The same should apply for religion and faith. Regrettably, our laws in Germany do not provide that freedom.

What Is a Sacrifice?

An area of pagan religions, which is often misunderstood, is the sacrifice. It is commonly believed that a sacrifice should appease or reward the Gods, say the transfer of the sacrificed goods should change the Gods' actions and behaviour. This notion is not completely wrong, but way too narrow and overlooks important basics.

Two further clarifications are necessary here. First, there are different kinds of sacrificial rituals, with different practices and different intentions. Most people with a Christian background will recognise those sacrifices connected with the destruction of something most valuable, be it objects or living beings, like a first-born from the herd or a bull. (We will call that form of sacrifice "destructional sacrifice" from now on.) Those sacrifices are often portrayed in the Bible and in Christianity they are deemed to be unnecessary due to the final and sustaining sacrifice of Jesus himself. Yet the New Testament does quote another kind of sacrifice, namely the consumption of sacrificial meat but it gives no details on the different intention of that form compared to the destructional sacrifice. It simply criticises it as improper and false idolatry (1 Cor 10).

Second, the religious, philosophical idea of the sacrifice goes far beyond the sole give and take between Gods and humans. It is simplified and misinterpreted as a payment, bribe or even magical influence on the Gods and that which would force them to specific actions.

Hans-Josef Klauck lists one normal and four special forms of Graeco-Roman sacrificial practices [Kla95]. The normal form of sacrifice is a slaughter with the following festive consumption of the edible parts of the sacrificed animal. Bone, fat and blood were given to the Gods. The same procedure was practised among the Germans, but we know that from archaeological findings in the so-called "sacrificial bogs" [Sim06a] rather than from written heritage. Even though the ancient satirists, such as Lucian, already mildly mocked that the Gods would receive nothing valuable that way, and they do not need it because they have nectar and Ambrosia for meal [Wer74], it is clear that it is an important celebration within the community to which the Gods are invited and honoured. The veneration of the Gods is not done by spending food, as a kind of payment, but instead by the offered participation in the feast.

The special forms are the oblation, the destructional sacrifice, oaths and covenants spoken and founded during a sacrifice, and the regalement of the Gods, the so-called *theoxeny*.

During an oblation food or drinks are actually given to the Gods, either completely or a portion of what was consumed by the participants.

In a destructional sacrifice the given subjects are literally completely destroyed, e.g. burned or damaged in way that they are no longer usable by humans, and afterwards sunk in a stretch of water or a bog or buried. This damaging was often practised by the Germanic peoples, especially when sacrificing weapons (see below) [Sim06a]. The Greeks and Romans practised destructional sacrifices less frequently, preferably as atonement or for Gods of the underworld. Sometimes food was sacrificed in that manner and mostly burned. But animals were usually properly slaughtered first; the burning of live-stock was rare.

In the ancient world wine or animals were sacrificed to affirm an oath, e.g. an oath of alliance. Sometimes human sacrifices were reported in this realm too, but those reports may rather be an outcome of political propaganda than reality. There is still a controversy among experts whether such a sacrifice was a ritual accompanying the oath and involving the Gods or rather had a magical purpose. The sacrifices could have been intended to illustrate or magically evoke a curse, which should affect those who will perjure or break the oath or alliance somehow in the future [Kla95].

The theoxeny is similar to the oblation but the Gods are invited to a table presenting the food as if it was an ordinary dinner instead of sacrificing the food or beverages directly. Then the food was probably mostly consumed by the priests or perhaps sacrificed in an oblation or destroyed later on.

In the present day, modern Paganism, the oblation is the normal form. Especially the *libation*, i.e. when a beverage is sacrificed, is often and gladly practised. The threshold to the destructional sacrifice is narrow, especially since libations are usually celebrated outdoors, often with a campfire, so that a burning of the offerings is self-evident. Feasts are also often connected with the rituals and practised in the antique pattern but a special or ritual slaughter is not common. If food is to be sacrificed it is quite normal to be bought in shops or supermarkets or self-grown in the case of vegetables.

It is often implied that the intention behind a pagan sacrifice is to move a God to certain actions. Among other reasoning, this is derived from the pagan-Roman saying *do ut des* = "I give that you might give". That someone sacrifices precisely for this reason, I do not deny, but the general meaning behind sacrifices is however far deeper.

An offering of thanks can of course be called a "deal", especially if it was previously promised a God in the hope that certain conditions may occur. But it is performed often enough due to unplanned or unexpected events so that the God who is deemed to be responsible for those events did the "deal" without any consultation or request beforehand.

The offerings of thanks are not listed as a special form in the above mentioned list. Any form of sacrifice can be an act of gratitude, an anticipatory gift, if a "deal" is intended, or simply a regular ritual action. Yet here you can see the difference in the intention. It does not simply reduce a sacrifice to be a gift made by humans to make a God compliant. Neither something automatic or even magical which they are compelled to react on. Of course, this strongly depends on the personal god-conception (see chapter WHAT IS A GOD?). One who regards gods as ideals or archetypes cannot enter into monetary bargains with them.

Personally, I deem a sacrifice to be a *symbolic* act in general, which points to an obvious worldly circumstance: You cannot reach anything without quid pro quo — no matter what it might be. Just to live, you have to breathe, eat and drink. For complex projects, you have to do more or invest, as an example, I mention learning.

One who wants to learn something, must spend time gaining knowledge and doing repetition, refraining during that time from other perhaps more pleasant things, and sometimes having to work through harrowing reading, formulas or models. Even though a lot of people will hold quite a different opinion than that, I am convinced that a sacrifice to a God will never wondrously produce the wanted knowledge or affect the result of a related exam.

Rather, the sacrifice is a symbol for the fact that the knowledge is not for free, that you must master it. A ritual dealing with that gives the ritualist a more stable state of mind regarding the desired changes. He can place himself in a better mental position through the rite of sacrifice in order to better perform in his tasks. The sacrifice itself has a positive effect but does not work in a superstitious way as other religious people or atheists might diagnose. Nevertheless, the divine influence in the context of the god-conception held by the ritualists can be identified here, thus a deeper meaning of the sacrifice ritual is given.

A certain malaise comes along if you might think that a more valuable sacrifice would have a larger effect. The sacrifices described in the myths (see below) may invoke this impression. A wealthy person could buy a better divine favour than the poor, which has often been criticised especially by the emerging Christianity. This criticism, of course, does not apply if the sacrifice is regarded as symbolism. The monetary value of the sacrificed goods then becomes secondary or even irrelevant.

As an alternative concept in Christianity it is proposed that a positive divine influence, such as grace, is a gift (e.g. see Eph 4:7 or 1 Cor 9:14f). Compared to this, the idea of being in a permanent state of give and take with the Gods, the divine, or the natural forces perceived in a religious sense, is quite different or even opposite. So, it is not surprising if today's common perception of a pagan sacrifice is a bit misguided. But if you look closer exactly this give and take between God and the people is also found in Christianity: Men must believe, refrain from sins or if the latter is not possible, remorsefully confess, regularly pray and join church service, and so on. Whether someone sacrifices such mental or physical gifts makes no difference to me; the idea behind the sacrificed good is more important than the nature of that good.

The exemplary interrelation between learning and necessary effort, as well as the reference to the sacrifice is shown in the myth of Mimir's Well [Jor01]. Odin has to sacrifice an eye to fetch wisdom form Mimir's Well. He does not lose his eye in a fight against ice giants as told in a Marvel movie [Mar12]. This myth is not about battle and war but about the hardship of gaining knowledge and wisdom.

Of course, this is not to be taken literally and thus be a prompt to sacrifice an eye to learn something. That would be exactly the wrong treatment of a myth. Here we have a symbolic narrative containing the teaching that nothing you want to achieve in your life is for free. This is true even for the Gods and even for the God of knowledge and wisdom when he learns something new. The travails of mankind are not made by the Gods nor are they a penalty devised by thcm, they experience them as well. Therefore, they are in any case a role model for your own dealings with adversity and hard-to-reach goals in life. If you regard the Gods as ideals (see page 53), then their essence as role models increases. The ritual sacrifice is a sign then, that you take this ideal seriously, that you give them gifts symbolising your own and the divine efforts.

The basic idea behind theoxeny and oblation with a connected subsequent feast of the celebrants is the invitation of the Gods into the celebrants own social community. The give and take, as suggested by the term sacrifice, is less important here than the gathering of mankind with the Gods or other higher beings. In theology this is called "Communion" and is not far away from the Holy Communion in Christianity. Food is also eaten there and Jesus is regarded to be present as well, whether real or symbolic depends on the denomination, although the philosophical foundation is somewhat different in Heathenism. For the process of the rite or the intention behind it, this makes only a tiny difference.

In pagan rituals the Gods are often invited, their entertainment is a hospitable act which makes it clear that the pagans form a quite normal community with the Gods. It is in no way different from common human communities. Especially in Nordic-Germanic

Paganism, this community is very close as the Gods and mankind are connected over the web of fate (see page 127). In a ritual with the invited Gods you practice exactly the same as you do in human societies: You come together to eat and drink, have fun, and exchange gifts. The cause and intention of this is more important than its financial value. This mutual give and take between friends is referred in the Hávamál [Poe12]: "Gift-givers' friendships are longest found."

To symbolically illustrate this in theoxeny and oblation is supposed to show that the Gods are not especially different kinds of companions than other people. You treat them like human companions or even as friends in order to emphasize the strong relationship. The actions in a ritual symbolise the ordinary interpersonal actions strengthening such a relationship.

When it comes to Nordic-Germanic Paganism, human sacrifice is still a widely discussed issue. It is often postulated, based on Roman sources and the lack of Germanic ones, that the ancient Germans practised it.

Archaeologically, there is hardly any supporting evidence. Only 88 human skeletons but tens of thousands of animal ones have been found at Germanic cult sites, mainly sacrificial bogs, which had been used for several centuries, even up to two millennia [Sim06a]. When statistically speaking alone, human sacrifices cannot have been customary. They were clearly not practised regularly, e.g. only on seasonal celebrations.

Other possibilities than sacrifice have been assumed based on the few findings. The corpses buried at the cult sites could have been criminals executed in a ritual way. A special rite was performed because the ancient Germans were afraid of *Wiedergänger* (= "raised from the dead") or other negative effects from the netherworld. Perhaps they died from unknown and frightening diseases or other reasons provoking such negative emotions, which urged the people to unusual burials.

What is the reason for the emphasis on Germanic human sacrifice in Roman texts then? Perhaps a Roman had witnessed such an unusual burial, interpreted it wrong and reported equally wrong on it. But more likely it is a response to the Germanic practice of sacrifice after a battle had been won. If an enemy unit, Roman or from other Germanic tribes, was defeated, all weapons and maybe all valuable goods of the opponents were ritually destroyed. Furthermore they did not take prisoners but killed all the defeated [Sim06a]. This has been accounted for several times in antiquity and during the Migration Period.

This practise had most likely a religious component. The sacrifices were probably intended to thank the Gods for the victory, and the Romans, for whom such behaviour was unthinkable, regarded it as a normal part of the Germanic religious life.

Now, this should be no excuse for the unnecessary killings, but they were not then an everyday religious practice as it is assumed, since they were carried out only in case of war. Death is already and always present there. Also remarkable is the sacrifice of the weapons as metal resources in Northern Europe were rather humble. Thus enormous financial value has been destroyed. Fighting battles to gain riches is hardly possible with this practise – except perhaps for territorial gains.

What Is Magic?

Religion is mostly seen as a belief in something supernatural, or with the definition preferred in this book it may be seen as the worship of the supernatural. Even if this will cause misunderstandings and controversies among many religious people, I personally do not believe in supernatural things or interactions at all; everything that exists is part of nature. This is fully compatible with an immanent god-conception by the way; immanent gods are also part of nature and therefore nothing supernatural. Thus religions with immanent gods can avoid any kind of belief in the supernatural without producing contradictions or nonsense in their teachings or mythological content.

Now then, everything which is part of nature obeys natural laws. It may sound strange to monotheists, religious people in general and atheists, but this also applies to immanent gods and is no contradiction to their adopted and revered attributes. Pagan Gods are subject to destiny and fate, the Germanic more than the Greek ones, and are neither omnipotent nor omni-anything Therefore they have limits set by natural laws.

Because magic has a high importance in the old and new Paganism, the question arises how it might fit into a world (or a world-view) that excludes anything supernatural. First we have to consider what is exactly meant by "magic".

Magical acts or rituals with abstruse results contradicting all natural laws are impossible if you do not accept supernatural effects. Chopping a post with an axe and then milking that post for milk, which among other absurdities was considered to be possible and a crime in the age of the witch trials [Hin89], is certainly and absolutely impossible in a naturalistic world-view.

To achieve such results by magical actions could, of course, be accomplished by natural effects and interactions yet unknown. Due to the given research situation, the probability of such causes is rather tiny and must be scientifically detectable according to the naturalistic world-view.

Another option is to declare naturalism itself to be wrong or inadequate, which is often done by religious ideologies. But if you look at all the successes of scientific exploration, which is based on naturalism as a philosophical premise, empirical measurements, tangible and permanent inspections of all its theories and continuous development, I deem its renunciation to be totally wrong.

Now, before the reader objects he has witnessed working magic rituals and before a naturalistic and scientific compatible clarification, according to the current state of scientific knowledge, will be given, I would like to describe an example from my own experience:

After a pretty serious accident I was lying in the hospital in the intensive care unit with numerous fractures, craniocerebral trauma and a few minor injuries. I learned that on a certain day in the near future a healing ritual performed by friends and acquaintances should take place several miles away. Exactly that day was the first day from which I could rise from bed again, walk around a bit and shower, and the latter with little help from the nurse. You can consider this a purely statistical coincidence, completely insignificant, or on the other hand assume a direct supernatural interaction. My explanation is that the mere knowledge of the point in time of the helping ritual put my mind into a state of being which stimulated the self-healing process. It stimulated it in such a way as to induce a quicker pace and provide positive results earlier.

The effect is achieved by the state of mind of the parties involved and not by obscure and physically non-measurable direct interactions. The effect may be positive or negative, depending on what is believed or thought to be the aim of the magic action – in the vernacular also called "white" and "black magic". This naturalistic effect functions on the participants exactly like the ones during the religious rituals described in the last chapter.

I like to call this effect the "mental placebo effect" because it pretty much matches the medical placebo effect, by which medicines without any real pharmacological effect have a clearly measurable healing effect on the patients treated with it [Uex08]. This is not limited to alleged medicine. It also functions on the attending doctor's or any other person's behaviour, which cannot have any medicinal effect but only a psychological one. If the medically senseless treatment appears very complex to the patient, i.e. difficult to learn and to practise so that only qualified personnel and no layman can perform it, he suspects an intended and existing effect. This is often seen in natural or shamanistic religions and helps in the same manner as useless drugs or applies damage if it is omitted and expected by the patient. For example, this can be the dance of a shaman or the formal visit of a doctor without any treatment or renewed examination.

One may now argue against this view that if you are not convinced by a "real" outcome, such rituals based on the placebo effect could not help yourself or be useful at all. It is plausible and comprehensible that the placebo effect, whether a medical or a magic one, mostly only helps people if they actually believe in the presence of a real outcome, and that it will fail as soon as they are aware that the effect is on a mental or spiritual level rather than a chemical or biological one. I would like to present three arguments against the notion that the knowledge of a certain placebo like effect must automatically lead to its failure:

First, I think that the placebo effect can work on you even if you know that it is a placebo simply if one is convinced at the same time that it works in general. The placebo effect works on a subconscious level. What some people consciously think of it may be insignificant and unimportant. As its effect is scientifically confirmed, there should be no doubt on the effect itself, rather on its external form or maybe its preparation in special cases. If form and means do not compel, the effect might not work at all. Now, rituals of a religion one follows deliberately are mostly compelling through their aesthetics and by their meaning. Therefore, there is nothing to be said against the practical and identifiable effects of the ritual on the psyche, health or other circumstances, even though a reductionist physical interaction is not present.

Second, in Paganism faith does not have the importance or significance as in some other religious forms. Here the actual implementation of the ritual or magical act matters, not faith in a particular effectiveness, which is not empirically detectable anyway. Keeping this attitude in mind magic can really work in the above sense without having to believe in supernatural effects.

Third and last of all, it applies especially in medicine, something counts as good and right, if it *helps*. The placebo does verifiably help and is thus useful. Why should there be any difference in the rest of your life and especially in the area of religion? Now this does not belong to the argument itself, but interestingly enough, the mere word "placebo" comes from a biblical Psalm dealing with the salvation of the soul from death performed by the biblical God: *Placebo Domino in regione vivorum* = "I will walk before the Lord in the land of the living" (Ps 116:9). The religious reference is already given in the very term itself.

Particularly in Christianity magic acts are considered to be per se evil, i.e. at least negative and not pleasing to God. This is historically connected with the massive witch hunts resulting from this attitude. Magic is something which Christians generally reject and heathens supposedly just practise because they generally reject Christianity – either because they are per se evil as well or simply irrational. No matter whether you accept a supernatural possibility for magic, regard it as rationally impossible, or treat it as a mental placebo effect that is compatible with and explicable by science, I think the Christian assessment of magic is nonsensical, since it is based on a very limited definition and conception of "magic".

In Christianity, there are also many ritual actions that lead to a result, which must be either based on a supernatural effect, on assumptions conflicting with the laws of nature, or on the pure mental attitude of the participants. The usual constraint made here to distinguish these rituals from magic is to limit the necessary supernatural operations to the Christian God alone, while in magic the human actor is the one accomplishing supernatural effect. This distinction causes logical problems, no matter whether magic is something supernatural or a mental placebo effect.

Whether a consecrated priest or an in whatever way initiated or trained magician leads a god to supernaturally act or puts your mind into the desired state by a ritual, makes no difference – neither theoretically nor practically. It is often argued then that a magician means to force a supreme being, which must not necessarily be a god, into action, while the Christian God voluntarily offers to act instead. This alleged difference is, of course, never empirically and objectively observable, and if you look at the following example, you will even see no theoretical basis for it. It is just a claim that has to be believed.

An example would be the Roman Catholic view on the process of the Eucharist during which the essence of bread and wine transforms into the body and blood of Jesus Christ. This is called *transubstantiation*, i.e. the conversion of the substance, which here does not mean the matter itself but its very essence or "Being" as such (οὐσία). The sensually perceivable form of bread and wine does not change [Mue77]. According to what we know of the structure of matter nowadays, this view is, of course, completely pointless, but that does not matter here – just as little as the philosophical foundations and implications do, for example, whether it must be understood in a Platonic or Aristotelian way.

What matters instead is the process of the ritual itself and the circumstances, which lead to its success. The transubstantiation is performed solely by the Christian God and only initiated by a priest by his words of consecration. Theoretically everyone could do that, even non-Christians, if that God responded positively to his words. No one relies on that hypothesis, however, and only the consecrated priest is understood to have a guarantee on an actual conversion. For the life of me, I cannot see how to distinguish between an always voluntarily or forced God responding to the priest's words. The same applies to the difference in principle between the conditions and necessities for the initiation into sorcery or those for the consecration into priesthood.

Let us then define the term "magic" a bit broader. First, by omitting the constraint that a certain divine act conjured by words should not be labelled as magic. And second, by revoking the idea that magic automatically sets processes in motion just like a natural law. In that case, we have something here which we can find in every religion.

Once the term is exempted from the belief in something supernatural or in yet unknown natural forces – while, as said before, I regard the first as impossible and the second as very unlikely –, you get a phenomenon that is scientifically proven and utilised in conventional every day medicine. There is for example the so-called "white-coat effect". Medicines and therapies verifiably help better if they are administered by someone in a white medical coat instead of casual wear or clothing of other professions [Reh05]. In our culture, the white coat belongs to the doctor's equipment, the patient's trust in a person administering medicine increases simply by the automatic categorisation as a studied doctor, and the treatment works better immediately. In the past, the white coat would have surely been seen as a magical accessory.

Besides the positive effect of the inculcated trust in familiar appearance, the exact same mental process may also cause negative health related results. One example is the increased blood pressure with measurements carried out by medical professionals in outpatient or inpatient care. Due to the nervousness of the patient, the values measured in this case are a little higher than those measured by the patient himself. A usual increase of 5 mmHg[9] is estimated here. Patients with a pronounced white-coat effect suffer from a significantly higher increase, the systolic one with an average of 27 mmHg, the diastolic 14 mmHg. This is known as "white-coat hypertension" [Kha07].

It is important here, that the person onto which the magic is supposed to work accepts the outer form and the means used. With a doctor it may be the white coat, in a prayer or summons, the proper text, even though neither the colour nor the textual content has any direct physical or pharmacological effect but only functions inside the cultural and sub-cultural notions of the "target person".

In my previously stated example, the healing ritual was not the only magic the mentioned pattern; it just made a great impression due to the chronological coincidence. There have been other rituals and prayers, even to Gods to whom I have no connection whatsoever. Perhaps the healing process would have in no way developed any differently without this mental and spiritual assistance. However, I perceived it as something very positive and I think it works in the manner described here, precisely because I knew that I

---

[9] millimeter mercury column, a vintage press ure unit

was not alone but received encouragement from so many friends and acquaintances.

Interestingly, exactly this pattern seems only sometimes or even often not to work with staunch Christians, as shown by a study of patients, whom have been prayed for [Ben06]. Those who knew of the prayer healed a statistically significant 14% worse off than those who did not. As an explanation for this reaction we can certainly exclude that those patients considered those prayers to be malicious, negative, or part of unacceptable magic in any sense. In the same issue of the cited journal Mitchell W. Krucoff has pointed out that the knowledge of a participation in a study in which one was prayed for due to his illness, led to an increased risk, because prayer implied a very dangerous and likely fatal disease [Kru06]. Personally, I can also imagine that psychological pressure was triggered in those people. The knowledge people are praying for them to an almighty and omni-benevolent God for assistance, urged them unconsciously to force said healing because it necessarily had to take place at that moment.

No matter what explanation may be true now, the exact same help, which led me and many others to a positive result, led them to a very negative one. I think the personal religious setting plays a huge role here. Depending on what attitude toward destiny, toward fighting against illness and death, toward solidarity with friends and relatives, as well as what expectations towards your Gods and such rituals or religious actions you have, it can certainly have a very different influence on the quality and the effectiveness of those rituals and actions.

Well, the area of magic is slightly broader defined than medical applications or other personal accomplishments. In modern Paganism, particularly the Germanic, "spirit journeys" and "shamanism" play a major role, both often closely related. Here as well, I consider supernatural or yet undiscovered physical interactions as less plausible, and the above stated explanation of how magic works also fits partially. It does not go so far as to include spirit journeys, and in shamanism aspects like herbal lore and botany have to be respected, both which have certainly real pharmacological effects and success in their medical application. This shall not be the content of this chapter, I only want to make some few, hopefully interesting, and I think important comments on both topics.

On a spirit journey the human consciousness travels a long way, visits other worlds and meets higher beings like the Gods themselves [Goo07]. Regarding how it works in reality the question arises whether the mind travels or the travel happens within the mind. Many will state the first, I tend to the latter.

Personal experience on a spirit journey may give quickly and clearly the impression, that one's own spirit actually leaves the body and embarks on a supernatural or scientifically not identified or identifiable way into far away realms of this world or some other. Such an out-of-body experience can be realised and enabled in different ways, by shamanic or magical rituals, by meditation and even by a technical intervention via magnetic fields calibrated in a certain way, such as neuroscientific experiments have already shown [Bla05]. Thus a pseudoscientific explanation such as an astral body and its actual travel is not really necessary. In terms of other worlds and any implications on a possible life after death the question arises as to how they could exist for real if visits there take "only" place in one's own mind — I refer to the next chapter for that topic.

On the subject of shamanism I would like to point out, that, contrary to the statements of some modern practising shamans or followers of shamanism, there is neither archaeological nor historical evidence, that our ancestors would have practised it in the way it is often done today. In my opinion, which I by the way share with one or two practising shamans, today's shamanism in European Paganisms is a latter-day syncretism from Siberian, other Asian and native American ideas which are connected with their respective Paganism as a religion. Out of the research in shamanism by Michael Harner the so called "core shamanism" has extracted and constructed [Har80]. This can be taken as a basis for the modern and private shamanism.

Especially the latter is often criticized [Noe99], but I think the fact, that today's shamanism in contemporary Paganism has no proven tradition and almost certainly differs from its historical counterpart, is by no means worthy of criticism. As long as you are aware you are following a neoshamanism [Wal03], and furthermore avoid persuading anyone, that you are standing in a historically proven and continuous tradition, there is nothing to speak out against pursuing such a path.

Strictly speaking the entire current Nordic-Germanic Paganism faces this dilemma. With a few exceptions, we practically know almost nothing historically evident about the actual sequence and wording of rituals, so that current practices are in fact new inventions to a large or even complete extent. But this is nothing bad or worrying, it is just imposed on us by fate and historical reality.

WHAT AWAITS US AFTER DEATH?

As an introduction to this chapter, I must first to mention that I am not so presumptuous as to claim I know exactly what happens to people after death or even if anything happens at all. We have nothing empirical or otherwise tangible in our hands. Even near death experiences, which I will discuss later, depend to a great deal on the culture a person is living in, and thus any assertion of certain knowledge about death coming from those sources would be inadmissible. Since everything that can be scientifically observed provides no indication of an afterlife, I would not even state I believed in or held a justified hope of a life after death. I would rather call it *wishful thinking*, which is by no means meant disrespectfully. This wishful thinking I want to expand on and sort into a possible range of pagan ideas. Today there are some prejudices and misperceptions misinterpretations on the ideas of our ancestors regarding the afterlife, which I would like to correct – mainly by presenting my views on the myths dealing with death, as historically secure knowledge is also scarce here. I will confine myself here to the Nordic-Germanic myths, for Graeco-Roman or others see e.g. [Cot08].

Let us have a look at the scientific and philosophical framework first. There is no empirical evidence of any form for some afterlife nor in general for a different plane of existence. This can be due to two reasons. Either there is no hereafter or we do not yet know how to observe it measurably. The latter allows for the possibility of its existence but at the same time denies any objective and general statements about it. In principle, the same problem applies here as we have already seen in the chapter WHAT IS ATHEISM?, The problem is of a non-measurable or unrecognisable god which inevitably leads to agnosticism regarding such a plane of existence. This does not automatically imply that you may not hope for nor have faith in such a thing.

Incidentally, the supposed existence of an afterlife contradicts neither the naturalistic world-view nor the conception of immanent gods. The yet undiscovered hereafter could be a normal part of a nature-like everything, including the Gods, no matter whether it was created by them or would have arisen by itself. In this context the term "multiverse"[10] is often mentioned, in which our universe and the hereafter are two universes in a larger cosmological structure. The whole cosmos would be that multiverse, not our universe alone, and the immanence of the hereafter and all entities living there, like the Gods or the dead, would still apply.

Apparitions and near death experiences (NDEs) are often seen as empirical evidence of an afterlife. To my knowledge there is no scientifically acceptable investigation that has observed apparitions, although explanations abound, how such appearances may occur without real ghosts. It is somewhat different with near death experiences. Here we have lots of studies that show astounding similarities such as light perception on the one hand but show enormous cultural differences on the other. The NDE's content, i.e. perceptions that could be indicative to the actual appearance of a hereafter, strongly depends on the culture the experiencing person was raised in and religious ideas he holds. Thus Christians often perceive paradise or hell, or angels and demons; Hindus may see cows. This can have two reasons. The simpler and perhaps more plausible one is that the brain remembers what it has learned in life about beliefs of the afterlife shortly before its death. On the other hand, there may be many otherworldly places, and the deceased arrive at one of them which is suitable – this idea is shown later in detail. A NDE may give a foretaste to those places. The often encountered light perception is in all cases probably just a purely neurobiological phenomenon and can be attributed to an increased carbon dioxide level in the blood stream [Kle10].

The next question is how a dead person or whatever part of him or her can get into the afterlife; a question to which different religions have different answers. Those answers range from consciousness and soul, which are not always the same, to complete physicality. The latter must be reproduced somehow as the worldly

---

[10] This has little to do with the multiverses hypotheses in physics such as the so called "many-worlds interpretation" [Car09].

body is surely not transferred somewhere else, at least not in its functioning form.

We encounter a fundamental problem here, namely how the human spirit, mind or soul is made up. There are mainly two philosophical concepts regarding body and mind, monism and dualism. A complete representation and discussion, as well as the notion of more detailed concepts are clearly outside the scope of this book. So I will only give a brief outline. For further reading, see e.g. [Kim05]. In addition to the above, you can also differentiate the mind or spirit into consciousness and soul. The consciousness is something physical and thus mortal, and the soul is something that can live on after death. The philosophical and theological implications are almost the same as in a pure dichotomy, thus the comments below about dualism match here as well.

In monism, the mind is either completely a part of the body or the other way round. That the mind consists of the structures of the body, essentially the brain, the neurons and hormonal activity, is common among naturalists and corresponds well to scientific observations. For obvious reasons, the latter view, that matter somehow consists of the mind, is also a monism but completely different than the first one and encountered only in rather strange philosophies and therefore rarely in scientific circles.

In dualism there are two separate entities, here the mind inhabits the body. Such a separate spirit is often considered to be supernatural, because there is no way to measure it in a scientifically accurate way. However, that may change in the future. The acceptance of a life after death is far easier and better with dualism than in monism. Here a dead body does not imply a dead spirit, as opposed to the monism with its "the mind consists of physical structures and actions" more or less automatically does. The spirit may survive a corporal death, even forever under certain circumstances. It is completely unclear scientifically how exactly the spirit inhabits the body and how it controls it. In monism that is not a problem[11], there mind and body form a single unit.

---

[11] Supposedly, in monism there is the so-called "Qualia problem". Subjective feelings cannot exactly be described by a physical mental

It is still unresolved how the transition of the human spirit from this world into the next really works, how the mind can leave the body and enter a different location, but with a dualism the sheer possibility seems much more plausible. Especially among naturalists and philosophical materialists with monistic ideas the conviction is common that, if the spirit is solely produced by neurobiological processes, its existence in a different place than the body must be impossible. However, if materialistic structures and processes form the mind in this world, it is theoretically possible that a mind can be formed by different but similar manners in other worlds. With regards to animism, this materialistic explanation of the mind implies the exact opposite of what we commonly conclude from it. If matter is capable of constructing the human mind, it is certainly possible that material structures can generally do this. Complex natural structures can produce a consciousness or a spirit. Other structures than human neurobiology would then probably produce alien forms of consciousness, even perhaps difficult or impossible for humans to recognise, but in principle the possibility exists. In the field of botany, an interdisciplinary field has been recently established, which deals with this subject in the plant kingdom – plant neurobiology [Bre06]. The assumption that objects could have a consciousness contrary to modern convictions that they cannot is, therefore, not a totally unscientific thought. Thus, it is not absurd as a naturalist to associate some consciousness with natural forces in a broader framework, although it is highly speculative and without any empirical findings.

Those structures could also be replicated. In modern speech this would be called a copy or a move of data. How this should work in detail is also unclear and unexplained. It is even more uncertain than with a dualistic mind, as it raises the question whether the person or soul itself and his or her self-awareness would still remain intact under such a process. Contrarily, a monistic mind is theoretically capable to travel into an afterlife for sure.

---

state and vice versa [Lew29], [Blo78]. I personally consider this objection to be nonsensical and not a valid argument for dualism.

Even though it was only meant as a scientific joke and therefore probably never tried, David E. H. Jones proposed a measurement some years ago which could physically demonstrate that the mind leaves the body in death [Jon95]. A prerequisite for this experiment is that a certain amount of energy is needed to maintain the information necessary to "build" an individual mind, which would be removed from the body in the moment of death and would be noticeable as a slight weight loss due to the equity of mass and energy. Practically, there are numerous objections that would make the whole project absurd such as the extremely low value of mass loss (evaporating sweat would have a much higher effect), and the determination of the exact moment of death.

Now we come to the notions on the afterlife in Nordic-Germanic Paganism. Neither the historical nor the modern notions are so clearly ascertainable or defined like many people believe – including for some of the followers of those notions.

There is a widespread public opinion that this hereafter is divided into only Valhalla and Hel, which is supposed to be a different form of heaven and hell. Only the warriors fallen in battle go to heaven, namely Valhalla, and all the rest go to hell. This view, derived from the Christian hereafter, contains so many errors in form and content regarding the mythological background. We shall try to put them straight now. For the mythological content in scripture see [Poe12] and [Sim06b]. Furthermore it contradicts the common paganistic philosophical ideas about the composition of the afterlife.

It is correct that the word "hell" etymologically descends from Hel. But this is more the name of the Goddess of Death rather than of the underworld itself. In German the name *Helheim* = "home of Hel" is quite common to distinguish the place Hel from the Goddess Hel. Hel is not an exclusive place of punishment, torture, or distance from God (or the Gods) as with the Christian hell. Opinions are divided whether Hel as a place is terrible or beautiful. Anyhow, the mythology states that Hel as a person has a beautiful and an ugly side, which symbolises the ambivalence of death as a possibly good or bad end of life. And since even dead Gods like Baldr end up there, Hel should not be an overly ugly place.

First, the dualistic separation of the hereafter into Valhalla and Hel, into warriors and everybody else is mythologically incorrect. The Eddas speak of three different places and if being very precise, of four. Those who have fallen in battle go to Asgard. Once there, Freyja selects the first half of them for herself and brings them to her palace Fólkvangr. Those left go to Odin's Valhalla. It's probably a matter of opinion, whether Fólkvangr or Valhalla is the more "exclusive goal", namely whether to reside in Odin's hall or be chosen by a Goddess is more desirable.

Those who die on the ocean, go into Ran's realm. Those who die by some other means, go to Hel. Besides the fact that in the myths the Nordic-Germanic hereafter is not that simple as many believe, it also has, of course, an effect on modern pagan conceptions of the afterlife and holds philosophical aspects regarding the process of dying which has some influence on how to live one's life.

The circumstance of the three different types of death determining to which location in the hereafter one might reach is often generalised in modern paganism. The concept is that there are many such places and your life, or how you live your life, determines to which of those you go after death. This could also be a very old concept, however, nothing substantial regarding it has been passed down from the old Germans. This is also not very far from the common Christian conceptions, only the number of possibilities available in them is far more limited and thus also the necessary conditions of your way of life. The core of this notion, which I personally consider to be extremely desirable by the way, is that you belong best to that God or those Gods fitting your own attitude to life, which is in my religious view the same thing anyway, even after death. Beyond that, I furthermore like the idea that you can travel around in such a hereafter shaped that way and visit all those places, the ancestors, the Gods and entities, with whom you would like to stick around with in an eternal life.

Those three types of death can (a bit poetically) be called "sword-death", "sea-death" and "straw-death". Just like the realm of Ran itself, the sea-death is often ignored in the public perception.

The sword-death is seen as the death in battle or war and the straw-death as the "standard" one, whereby the first is the honourable one for warriors and the latter the dishonourable one for all other people. I have a clearly different view on that topic and give three reasons against the previously stated ones, a cultural-historical, a mythological-content and a philosophical one suitable for a personal attitude and way of life.

From a cultural perspective one has to first keep in mind in which historical period the myths had been written down. The target audience back then was less the common people than the noble ruling class, who were just warriors. That warriors make a better impression than the rest should not, when superficially regarding the hereafter, be treated as a general rule for the way of life and its consequences for a life after death.

In general the content of the myths should not be taken literally. This applies especially for the everyday life of a fallen warrior in Valhalla, as told in the Grímnismál (Sayings of Grímnir). In this story, Odin visits his protegé king Geirröth under the guise and name of Grímnir , to test and learn whether he is an honourable man or indeed, a níðing [Wik12c], i.e. someone who mistreats his guests, as claimed by his wife Frigg. Grímnir is a guest in Geirröth's hall, is indeed mistreated by him, and tries to show him with many stories becoming more and more obvious, to whom he is refusing hospitality. Grímnir gets nothing to eat, only something to drink, and he has to sit between two fires, both very close to him. He talks about Valhalla, where Odin eats nothing, only drinks mead, and where a soot-blackened cook called Andhrímnir = "sooty" or "the soot-blackened" prepares the meals for the warriors. Both situations are very similar. In my opinion Grímnir is showing Geirröth, that in fact Odin is sitting in front of him, and he is not literally describing the warriors' afterlife. Thus, one should be very cautious if one treats this imagery as the actual viewpoint of the hereafter at that time.

Due to the few sources, it is by no means clear what conception of the hereafter our ancestors really and precisely held. The diplomat and envoy Ibn Fadlan reported in the 10th century on the notions of the Rus, a Nordic tribe, in which in the afterlife one meets one's ancestors and all the members of one's house [Fry05] at a place, which today is often called the "hall of the ancestors". He quotes a slavegirl's prayer at her lord's funeral that was also used as a basis for a scene in the movie "The 13th Warrior" [Imd12]: "Behold, I see my father and mother. There I see all my deceased relatives sitting. There I behold my lord sitting in paradise, and paradise is fair and green, and around him are men and servants. He calls me; bring me to him."

A story handed down about the Frisian king Radbod points in the same direction [Nea43]. Radbod asked bishop Willibrord about his intended and practically started baptism, with one foot already in the holy water, whether he would meet his ancestors in heaven. To the reply that they will surely be damned to hell, as they were all heathens, he refused the baptism and conversion with the statement that he would rather stay in hell with his relatives than with strangers in heaven. He kept the religion of his fathers.

Perhaps the heathen ancestors had no concrete conceptions on the afterlife, which is often stated as a reason for the attractiveness of the upcoming Christianity with its very precise view. Thus, in the 8th century, the Christian monk Bede[12] put the following words into the mouth of a noble heathen, whereby the phrase "the new teaching" was supposed to mean Christianity [Sim06a], [Her13]: "You sit at supper in winter, with your commanders and ministers, and a good fire in the midst, whilst the storms of rain and snow prevail abroad; the sparrow, I say, flying in at one door, and immediately out at another, whilst he, who is within, is safe from the wintry storm; but after a short space of fair weather, he immediately vanishes out of your sight, into the dark winter from which he had emerged. So this life of man appears for a short space, but of what went before, or what is to follow, we are utterly ignorant. If, therefore, this new

---

[12] The same monk mentioned the pagan Goddess of spring *Eostrae* [Bed43], which Jacob Grimm translated into the German *Ostara* [Gri35] and both derived "Eastern" (*Ostern*) from it. Bede and Jacob triggered the still-simmering dispute whether the ancestors actually knew this Goddess. I say the awakening of the spring is so beautiful, even a completely new and quite modern Goddess of spring is adorable.

doctrine contains something more certain, it seems justly to deserve to be followed." The worldly life is only a short period in an unknown surrounding, the warmth in a cold winter. To what extent Bede quoted a historical heathen, described a common opinion, or only did some missionary propaganda is impossible to decide due to missing comparative pagan sources. I consider it highly likely though that such a view was a frequent and common one back then. It would surely justify why Heathenism, no matter whether at that time or nowadays, is more concerned with this world than the next one. The life here and now is well known, one concentrates on that one and towards it alone one develops an attitude, a feeling, a style and acts together with the Gods in rituals for occasions, that happen here and now – *do ut des*. What comes after death is by far more uncertain. You cannot really prepare for it, as religions concentrating on the hereafter do by faith or rites. The view that the worldly lifestyle has some influence on thc possible next life is not given up though. The three types of death show that the circumstances and possible goals are however far more flexible and complex.

In my opinion there is more behind those three types of death than just dying in battle, on the ocean, or somewhere else. They are simple names for certain different situations in which you can die, and the personal attitudes towards death and dying from which a philosophy can be drawn. The sword-death is not about battles and wars but about fighting against your death and the incipient circumstances such as an illness, for example. He who fights an illness holds no sword as a weapon but medicine instead and he does not go to a battlefield but to therapy. It is about not simply accepting your pending fate, your imminent death, but to fight against it.

Now the sea-death is an accident, a sudden stroke of fate that is not predictable, not foreseeable and thus not combatable. This does not need to happen on the sea; today it is more likely on the highway, at work, or during housekeeping.

The straw-death, the dying in your bed, describes the fatalistic acceptance of death – in the case of an illness, for example, to hang on the wires and tubes awaiting death. This prospect still discourages many today and they try to prevent it happening with a patient's provision. From that point of view this former perception of death does not differ from the modern ones, it is only expressed in different words.

So the three mythological ways of death describe the three possibilities of dying by fate. The sword-death is in opposition toward an unwanted destiny, the sea-death is the unforeseen and thus unavoidable stroke of fate, namely an accident, and the straw-death is the fatalism of those who have resigned. The latter handling of fate is not desirable in Germanic Heathenism, ergo the straw-death is not desirable, and you try to live in a way that it ends in a sword- or sea-death. The next chapter deals with the handling of fate in more detail.

How does suicide fit into this pattern? Does it fit in at all? With a suicide you are not struck by fate but by your own will. The Stoics thought that destiny is the same as the divine will and thus determined and unchangeable; and suicide was man's only option to be free from fate. Seneca wrote in *De Consolatione ad Marciam* [Kla96]: "But I also see death… It is not unbearable to be a slave, as it is possible to get to freedom in one single step." You can interpret this as fighting against fate and thus diagnose a sword-death, even though this surely does not apply to every suicide, if you look at the psychological surroundings causing them. The Nordic-Germanic myths however emphasise that you should always try to live and carry on, even if you are threatened by adverse circumstances or physical deficiencies. This is assuredly connected to the worldly focus of Nordic-Germanic Heathenism. The Hávamál says on that topic [Poe12]: "It is better to live than to lie a corpse. […] No good can come of a corpse."

It is important though, as it was to our ancestors, that the following generations would remember and honour one's deeds and accomplishments. The consequences of your own completed actions, no matter how insignificant or already forgotten they are, have indeed happened and cannot be cancelled. The acting had an effect on the web of fate and is thereby in a sense eternal, no matter whether there is a real life after death or not. The Hávamál contains a nice verse on that topic [Poe12]:

Cattle die, and kinsmen die,
And so one dies one's self;
But a noble name will never die,
If good renown one gets.
One thing now that never dies,
The fame of a dead man's deeds.

As mentioned before, missing scientific evidence and clues make it impossible for me to regard a hereafter being likely, to believe in it, or to be firmly convinced of its existence. From all that mankind has empirically observed I think and presume that the life after death feels pretty much the same as the one before procreation. That neither makes me glad or unhappy; you can regard it as simple non-existence, the unknown, or the sparrow in winter outside the hall (see above). If death is the final end of our existence, it is a destiny we cannot escape. If that, which awaits us, is totally unknown and we can actually do something about it, then we do not precisely know how nor what to do, and could only listen to people who pretend to have discovered the unknown.

Nonetheless, I do wish beyond all measure to meet my loved ones again in the hall of our ancestors, to roam Vidar's green lands together with the Silent One, or to travel the Nine Worlds and discover all kinds of new things. Unfortunately a wish does not produce reality. But the desired and wished for shape or pure existence or non-existence of the afterlife should have no influence on your own way of life. The already mentioned worldly orientation of Paganism reflects this quite well in my opinion. The either desired or unforeseen or unwanted way of dying refer only to the way of life in this world, as long as your regard the places in the afterlife as mythological symbols rather than exactly described locations or circumstances. It also refers to life itself – its last moment – and not to death or whatever may happen afterwards.

And perhaps the truth about the afterlife is what other religions imagine or pretend. In East Asia the view is common that the soul does not leave the Earth but travels to a different location. In Shintoism it may become a natural spirit after the corporal death and inhabit a shrine. To live in a forest as a *kami* would definitely suit me.

Or maybe the Hindus and Buddhists are correct and we go into Nirvana or make another round on the wheel of life. That does not sound so bad to me.

Or perhaps there really is a benevolent, just and all-knowing God that moderate Christians are always talking about, despite my conviction that this is logically and empirically impossible. Then he will surely know on judgement day that I did not refuse him because of obduracy or malignity but for quite different reasons as mentioned in this book, and we will get along somehow.

Or there is a vengeful and jealous God as imagined and believed in by the fundamentalist monotheists, who tortures and agonises anyone, who is not beholden to him or worship him in the exact way laid out in his holy scripture. Then I would rather stick to king Radbod's view and spend the eternity in hell with decent people than in heaven with those beings.

There is an interesting difference between the Protestant and Catholic concept of the hereafter, by the way, which makes the Catholic one by far more logical and ethical. Namely the purgatory , which I deem inevitable if there really is the just and simultaneously benevolent God who the Christian one is supposed to be. In the Protestant concept one arrives at the moment of death or judgement day – the exact point in time is unclear and depends on the denomination and interpretation – at an otherworldly selection ramp where it is decided whether one goes to heaven or hell. A faithful mass murderer, who repents ten seconds before his death, may enter heaven, whilst an infidel, who has stolen chewing gum once and feels sorry about it, goes to hell for eternity. That is neither just nor benevolent. In purgatory, however, you are punished according to the seriousness of your crimes and sins and may reach heaven afterwards, if all the remaining conditions are fulfilled. I know that there are Protestants and Catholics who postulate an empty or an eventually empty hell or leave the last decision on the eternal future of the deceased to their God, rather than a simple human rule based on the influence of the faith by itself. But the Catholic mythology has a better ethical basis here in my opinion.

There are countless possibilities which await us after death, including the absolute end and vanishing of our consciousness. Only one, the last one in the above stated list, with all the torturing by a jealous god, sounds really bad to me. What is evidently going to happen, escapes my knowledge and I do not dare to make a prediction. But we cannot change it anyway, because it is either an unavoidable fate or so inscrutable that we simply lack the option of a predictable action. Therefore, we should not have gloomy thoughts or feel sorrow about it, i.e. for yourself. That you feel concern for loved ones, friends and relatives, while they live, and miss them, when they are dead, does not contradict a relaxed rapport to death.

To finish this chapter I would like to present two quotes with a pagan background, which may free us from the fright and concerns around death:

> "Thc allegedly most terrible of all evils, death, is nothing to us, since when we are, death has not come, and when death has come, we are not." (Epicurus, [Kla96])

> A measure of wisdom each man shall have,
> But never too much let him know;
> Let no man the fate before him see
> For so is he freest from sorrow.
> (Hávamál , [Poe12])

Why I Am a Heathen.

Let us now come to my reasons and explanations why Paganism, especially the Nordic-Germanic one, is so fascinating and a religion worthy to follow. First I would like to cover my religious development from childhood until today, since this will explain a lot about my motivation and will provide some insight into the reasons behind it. I will make some remarks about Christianity and what I do not like about it, as many of my reasons are based on an opposition to Christianity. Of course, that subset of reasons explains only why I am not a Christian rather than why I am a heathen, but they are still essential to understand my development and world-view.

I grew up in a half atheist and half Protestant family, neither of them was imparted as an ideology. I was not told, the Christian God existed nor was I told the opposite. Rituals were not celebrated and we never went to church. We had a New Testament but no complete bible at home. My grandmother was very Christian and very active in her parish but never missionary minded. Jehovah's Witnesses came frequently to her door, so I had the Watchtower and something alike as literature. Now, the theological basis of their faith is rarely accepted in society and their bible translation differs a bit from others. Their views are indeed fundamentalist but their mythological stories are exactly the same as those of the bigger Christian currents. That constellation spared me the otherwise usual religious indoctrination during childhood, which can only be rarely escaped or escaped with difficulty later. I was simply indifferent to the Christian religion and faith; I was neither explicitly in favour nor against it.

I was baptised though, had religious classes in school and had to undergo the confirmation. Thus I learned the Christian, in more detail the Protestant content of faith from official sources but never really believed in it.

There are some amusing and partly ironical anecdotes from my school and church education, which shed some light on my later steps and development. I cannot really remember the religious education in primary school. I think they taught the usual biblical stories of the creation, the Flood, the Exodus and the important events in the life of Jesus, e.g. his birth, the Sermon on the Mount, his resurrection, etc., but all that may be scenes from a clouded memory. In the 5th and 6th grade we only memorised prayers and songs; the teacher was a priest. Starting in the 7th grade I received instruction from a very committed evangelical teacher, who taught me a lot on Christian ethics.

One day he told us about Boniface, whom he claimed to be a courageous hero and convincing missionary who showed the stupid heathens in Fritzlar how powerless their Gods were by felling the holy Donar Oak belonging to the Chatti. The fact that thereupon he was not killed by lightning, not immediately felled himself, was supposed to be clear evidence how right the Christian and how wrong the heathens are. Even as twelve-year-old boy I could not accept that and was pretty sure, that no immediate divine judgement will hit me, if I burned down a church, and that such an action would convince Christians more of my malignity and not of my righteousness and honesty. If I tell that to Christians today, they often reply that back then the pagans did believe the nonsense of immediate divine revenge and Boniface did disprove that belief. Even if the pagans had such a faith, the argument is not really convincing to support converting, since especially Christians with their otherworldly heaven-hell-dualism believe in a delayed divine punishment for such crimes against their own relics and sanctuaries. Usually you do not learn in school or church that Boniface's courage was not nearly as big as his missionary eagerness and that he was protected by a Frankish squadron stationed nearby in Büraburg while desecrating said oak. He first travelled without a military escort in his later days when he wanted to die a martyr's death by committing similar crimes in Frisia. For all that you need to read relevant historical literature or his biography written by Willibald [Rau94].

The same teacher told a allegory about active help, its ethical value and why one has to render it because of charity. It was about the offertory after a service where a poor old woman gave 10 pfennigs and a rich man gave 100 marks (the € did not yet exist at that time). One should regard the donation of the poor woman to be much more ethical than the one of the rich guy. She owned almost nothing and gave nonetheless; he had enough, so a larger offering had no reputation. The poor woman certainly exerted herself far more than the rich man in financial terms, but I do not see, or to be more precise, accept the sense behind that story.

The idea that a poor person who exerts himself more financially is more ethical than a rich person who helps, is easy to understand but also counterproductive. First, the rich man is donating exactly a thousand times more money than the poor woman. That does not make him a thousand times more ethical, but you can buy a thousand times more stuff from his donation, which helps a thousand times more. And it does not belittle the charity of the poor to regard the help of the rich as proper help either. One should be happy about the help from such large sums instead of calling the donor ethically inferior. Second, this attitude can lead to precarious consequences. If being poor and helping is generally better than being rich and helping, why not just ruin yourself financially like the old women did? You would be the better human being with a better prospect for the afterlife. At the end of the day a rich man shall hardly enter into the kingdom of heaven (Matt 19:23). However, the number of needy people will constantly rise then, whilst those who can actually and effectively help will diminish and perhaps even vanish some day. You cannot create or maintain a social society or system that way.

At the same age I attended a two-year course preparing for confirmation. Even though I did not treat the Flood or the resurrection as historical events, I developed a faith there in the Christian God which rested on the consideration that all stories and revelations could contain some truth and, therefore, it would do no harm to treat that god with respect and worship him. Especially when you think about the possibility of what could happen to you after death. Years later I learned that this was a simpler, but by no means stupider version, if you ask me, of the so-called "Pascal's Wager", which the mathematician and inventor of the Roulette Blaise Pascal formulated in the 17th century and which was always totally absurd [Pas99]. This wager pretends to be a statistic proving faith in God was the better option. If you believed and he existed, you won by going to heaven. If you did not believe and he existed, you lost by going to hell. If he did not exist at all, it did not matter whether you believed or not, as in death you disappeared anyway. There are so many logical errors in this consideration, more than I want to explain here, starting with the circumstance that you in fact already believe in the Christian God if you accept the Christian hereafter as a basis for such an argument. You wrap up arguing about the complete ignorance towards the possible existence of other Gods or hereafters. Perhaps there is an afterlife without any god or maybe some other god exists and prefers people who do not believe in him over those who have faith in the wrong Christian one.

At the end of the confirmation there was an exam on the curriculum in which two friends and I nearly failed, because two elders claimed we had not said anything. But the priest did hear and listen to our contribution, so that cup passed from me. During the confirmation I received the following saying (1 John 5:4): "This is the victory that has overcome the world, even our faith."[13] Today I believe, as martial as it sounds, it would befit Mars or Tyr too.

The confirmation is usually seen as the wilful acknowledgement and irrefutable confession of your own Christianity, as you could not do that at the time of your infant baptism. If you ask me today, how I could do that and still turn away from the faith that I shared (although not dogmatically), I often answer for the fun of it: "I was young and needed the money."

I never gave any thought to the idea that the Christian myths were historical events. Already as a child I was very interested in astronomy[14] and almost everything you learn from it contradicts the stories in the Old Testament, if they are taken literally. The sequence in Genesis, the Flood, the Exodus and similar things are simply impossible in the real universe. The alleged history in the

---

[13] This might be a bit confusing and does not mean, the victory has even overcome our faith but it is the faith that has overcome the world. In German or the English Standard edition the word "even" is missing.

[14] Due to my astronomical interest I also never understood why red should be a "warm" and blue a "cold" colour. Blue stars are much hotter than red ones [Ree11].

New Testament is not about cosmology but deals with the life of Jesus. Virgin births, chanting demons into a herd of pigs, arousing the dead or magically fixing an ear, however, seemed a bit far-fetched for me, even as a child, to regard those happenings as historical facts. Not every Christian nowadays treats everything written down in the bible as literal truth but they cannot actually avoid it with some of the episodes, at least not with the resurrection.

After confirmation and with growing scientific knowledge I soon had enough of Christianity and removed myself from the religious courses in school. This is granted by the German constitution. I was the first one in my grade and had to attend parallel classes. As soon as enough other pupils had joined we were organised into a separate class. Unofficially it was called "heathen supervision", which of course referred to the atheistic interpretation of the term "heathen" and did not relate to antique or modern Paganism. Most of those who skipped religious education at my school were members of smaller Christian movements, such as the New Apostolic Church or free evangelical churches. For them the instructions provided by the two big denominations allowed to teach were perhaps not fanatical enough. Only a manageable number were atheists.

When I reached the age of consent, I withdrew from the church. At that time I lived in a parish called *Heide*, which of course referred to the heathland not the religious orientation (the German word *Heide* means both, "heath" and "heathen"). Coincidence or destiny? The readers may judge for themselves but I think it is quite funny.

For quite a while I was a hardcore atheist, the Christian God was impossible by nature and I applied that notion to every religion there is, i.e. I made exactly the same error I explained and criticised in the previous chapters. The many religions are so diverse and their concepts and faiths so different that treating them equally and exactly the same as Christianity is simply wrong. This is common due to the lack of public interest and the resulting lack of knowledge in general. I was and I still am a naturalist, I do not believe in anything supernatural and I never have. That did not match with religion at all. I thought religion is always and generally connected to the supernatural and contradicts the natural sciences in every way.

I did not know the ancient definition formulated by Cicero yet (see page 16). Furthermore, I believed every religion in principle possessed an absolute and exclusive truth which they proclaim. Thus, statistically speaking, none of them could be true due to their absolute mutual exclusiveness.

Initially I wanted to study astronomy but I eventually changed to physics. They are not that distant from each other. Over the years I have heard many philosophical and scientific statements from the last two and a half millennia supporting my atheist views, such as the theodicy [Lei10], the impossibility of omnipotence and omniscience [Rus18], or the fact that the content of almost any myth in this world cannot be true by scientific standards. Already at the beginning of those two and a half millennia Xenophanes wrote about the anthropomorphised images of the Greek Gods drawn by Hesiod and Homer [Xen88]:

"But mortals deem that the Gods are begotten as they are, and have clothes like theirs, and voice and form.

But if cattle and horses and lions had hands or could paint with their hands and create works such as men do, horses like horses and cattle like cattle also would depict the Gods' shapes and make their bodies of such a sort as the form they themselves have.

Ethiopians say that their Gods are snub-nosed and black Thracians that they are pale and red-haired."

Today Xenophanes is often quoted as an early atheist, but he criticised only the literal conception of manlike Gods and was actually more a monotheist than an atheist.

I read the entire bible during that time and just maybe I skipped some of the page-long genealogy. As said before, the number of Christians, who interpret everything in the bible literally, is low, but at the very least large parts of the gospels, especially the resurrection, are commonly accepted as historical events and children are taught exactly that. Theology at the university may be more sophisticated, but in my experience the common believers do not benefit or even hear about it; they are deliberately kept in ignorance about the complex theological aspects – out of laziness or ill intent. Therefore, I regarded the biblical stories as myths at that time, as I do today. That most of the biblical stories cannot be historically true should be obvious to anyone who has a certain degree of school education. Why their teachings and statements, with a few exceptions, should bring anything positive, I have never understood – neither back then nor today, but more on that topic later.

In my Protestant environment Catholics were always regarded to be a bit superstitious. Although they had the same faith, they had enlarged its original scope with the cult of Mary, the veneration of saints and unnecessary pomp. I always thought this view was strange and wrong. Protestant and Catholic faith are nearly identical, the tiny little differences do nothing which would make an impression on an infidel. Judging from my own anecdotal experience, the Protestant morale is, except for the evangelical ones, statistically less narrow-minded and bourgeois than the Catholic one. The Catholic theology, however, is far more acceptable than the Protestant one. A good example is the purgatory mentioned in the previous chapter. The Protestant[15] iconoclasm has ensured that Protestant churches are less handsome than Catholic ones. Nowadays I have to admit that things like the cult of Mary and the veneration of saints are a beautiful reminiscence to polytheistic times, which I do approve – not regarding their content but their outer shape. From the Protestant and Islamic point of view this is a common critique on Catholicism while it is, of course, vehemently rejected in Catholic circles. The cult of Isis is clearly a role model for the cult of Mary. The iconography is almost identical and Mary has inherited many of Isis's titles such as the Star of the Sea (*stella maris*), Godmother and Queen of Heaven [Wik12b].

I always found it strange as well that Protestantism was supposed to be closer to original Christianity than Catholicism or Orthodoxy. This was just because of the temporal distance of its foundation and its focus on scripture which was compiled by exactly those people whose denomination was rejected. The

---

[15] Historically the protest in "Protestantism" was not against the pope or the Catholic church as many suppose, but against the planned repeal of decisions regarding religious freedom (as it was interpreted back then and decreed on the *Reichstag* in Speyer 1526) by emperor Karl V. in 1529 [Rab89].

arguments presented by Protestants to make themselves more originally Christian than their competitors looks like a conspiracy theory to me. I often say, the usual amount of superstition suffices to be a Catholic; a Protestant needs some paranoia in addition to that.

From reading the bible, from the Corinthian letter I have memorised as a favourite and perfectly fitting to my attitude: "But we preach Christ crucified, to the Jews a stumbling block and to the Greek foolishness." (1 Cor 1:23)

(Although unnecessary in the original German edition, that verse needs some further explanation here due to the differences between the English and German bible translations. Christianity started with a half Jewish and half non-Jewish background. The non-Jewish part is called "gentiles" and means the non-Israelite part of the world, which was the Roman Empire back then. "Greek" refers to the Greek culture adopted and adhered by the ruling Romans. Martin Luther translated *Heiden* = "heathens" instead of "Greek". Thus in Luther's words the Jews are angry about Christianity and we heathens think it is foolish.)

In my atheist phase I was never opposed to the faith of other people or their rituals, stories and celebrations, even though I did not share in them. My opposition was against the theocratic influence of the big state churches, which according to our constitution do not exist and may therefore not be labelled as such. I am against the abuse of rights, the lack of separation of state and religion, and the permanent effort to force a faith upon you, to which you do not agree because of its dogmas, contents and views. Nevertheless, I have always loved to read myths and sagas, especially the Greek and Nordic ones. The interest in the complex of themes was always there.

I also took often part in diverse religious rituals. Among them were public Shinto feasts, but I must admit I did not understood hardly anything, and they seemed like local folk festivals to me. Anyway, one was allowed to participate without any precondition. It was of no interest to anyone if you really belonged to the religion or had faith in anything they believed in.

I went to a Buddhist temple festival and did some fire-walking like everybody else there. To walk on glowing charcoal is often sold as a supernatural ability over here, which can be learned for a lot of money in esoteric lectures. In fact, nothing bad happens to a foot well supplied with blood due to the very small thermal conduction between the coal and the top layer of skin during the short contact time of marginal pressure to the sole. I have had black feet for four weeks but no visible burnings or pain. The monks, who walked over the coal first, may have felt slightly more pain. The important thing is to walk steady and quickly to minimise the contact period, not to run, which would increase the pressure and whirl up the coal, and not to be nervous. The latter prohibits mistakes you may make, that would increase the potential risks, and probably improves the blood circulation which carries some of the conducted heat away. That process also mitigates the risk of burning yourself. Meditation and rituals naturally do help here to lower the nervousness and to reach the correct mental state, a complete trance or faith in anything supernatural, esoteric or occult teachings is not necessary. Unshakeable "faith" in the "truth" of the thermal conductivity differential equation did work very well for me.

I wore a Thor's hammer earlier, not for religious reason but as jewellery. Perhaps it has evolved from the club of Hercules which the Franks already wore as amulets and may point to the identification of Thor and Hercules made by Tacitus. In former times, the hammer was probably only worn by women [Sim06a], a fact that is today often used as a critique or reproach against hammer wearing men. In that case, I reply we live in the age of emancipation, where men may do things that were formerly reserved for only women.

Of course, I participated in Christian services as well. During the confirmation lessons we were obliged to visit church on Sundays. Afterwards, I went to baptisms, weddings, funerals of friends, relatives and acquaintances or even to openings of the local shooting festivals. The above mentioned occasions never triggered a spiritual or emotional response in me.

This changed, when a good friend asked whether we could do a heathen ritual on our land accompanying an Easter bonfire. In our rural area a bonfire is allowed to be performed privately by anyone who declares it to the administration, applies the necessary security measures and offers access to the public. My wife and I agreed. We knew that some of our friends had found a home in Paganism and we gladly joined the celebration. The rules behind that celebration were simple. There was nothing to first learn or to practise. But this sole ritual caused a lot of positive emotions, something I had never felt before in a religious context.

It was not really spontaneous or immediately convincing but I was introduced to new people and got the chance to discuss modern Paganism with them. I was still stuck in the fallacy that all religious people must literally believe in the contents of their myths and wondered how someone could be that way with old pagan stories in modern times. Especially after the age of enlightenment, several scientific paradigm shifts and enormous cultural and technical progress. At the cosy get-together after the ritual I asked one of the newly acquainted about this problem and got the following answer: "It is not important what you believe but what you honour." This very close to Steinbock's statement [Ste04] quoted on page 26 and inspired me to think twice.

The idea of beholding the Gods as personifications of venerable ideals and as an incontestable innate natural phenomena rather than transcendent and supernatural entities, which was impossible in my naturalistic world-view anyway, was convincing to me. The same applies for the fact that the concept is not new but was already described by ancient authors and within the myths themselves, i.e. if you liberate them from pietistic superstition and atheist rejection. It is not about a dogmatic, absolute truth and a faith uncompromised by contradicting scientific facts. It is about personal philosophy and a way and attitude towards life.

In pagan religions it is usually not a problem to worship Gods from other religions or cultures, as it is not a matter of dogmatic faith what pantheon has to be venerated. The personal decision which pantheon suits you (or why you suit it) does not depend on what or how you have to believe but how it fits emotionally and spiritually to the above mentioned attitudes. I noticed that Nordic-Germanic Heathenism matches nearly exactly my ideas and attitudes regarding ethics, morale, values, virtues and the handling of fate. Its imagery holds in its mythological form a world-view I already had before without a religion. Something like a conversion, reversal or complete change in your life, as often required in monotheisms, was not necessary and would not have been appealing.

I can accept and worship Gods from other myths just as I do with my "own" Gods, e.g. some of the Greek Gods. There are only slight differences in character, behaviour and associated world-view, but those differences make the Nordic-Germanic Gods more interesting and more venerable to me. An extreme example would be the Christian God, who could also be seen as a personified ideal and natural force or, better stated, a sum of all of them. Most Christian would probably not agree to that though. The logical and scientific problems in the assumption of a creator existing before the cosmos have already been discussed. Now, let us take a look at his character and the ideals embodied in his mythical actions.

I was never able to understand how someone could admire the God of the Old Testament in particular. At least on four different occasions he kills innocent children or those with only slightly bad manners. There is the Flood (Gen 6), the under-age inhabitants of Sodom and Gomorrah (Gen 19), the murder of all the Egyptian firstborn (Exod 11), and the 42 young men because they mocked the prophet Elisha for being bald-headed (2 Kgs 2:23f). The story of Sodom and Gomorrah has another interesting facet beside the slaughter of all those allegedly horrible sinners and besides the woman who should have been saved if she had not looked the wrong way. The faithful and honourable Lot, who is deemed worthy to be saved, offers his virgin daughter to a mob to be raped because said mob are molesting two mighty angels. Those angles would surely be able to defends themselves and avoid any mischief.

Of course, those stories never really did happen. And even if parts of them were true, like the downfall of two ancient cities, no higher being would have accomplished that in the exact way it is told. The question remains: What is going on in the mind of someone, who thinks an entity with such a mythological behaviour is the source of love, morale and justice, especially if he assumes a historical accuracy behind those stories?

The concept of God changes with the New Testament, however, I face the same problem with almost all of the statements made by Jesus. The statements which our society teaches as being ethically and morally valuable. An often cited example is the stoning of the woman caught in the act of adultery. Only those without sin should cast a stone, there is nothing about the possibility that the death penalty for adultery might be a bit excessive or adultery should perhaps not be a criminal act. Following the same logic, a judge, who once drove 5mph too fast on a highway, may not put a murderer in jail.

In my opinion, there are three passages in the gospels in which Jesus says something wise and meaningful about behavioural norms. They fit into my ethical system too. Strangely those norms were rarely seen among Christians and other monotheists in general. At first there is the mote and the bean (Matt 7:3; Luke 6:41). You should not criticise others for things you are doing yourself all the time. There are religions in this world that react very indignantly, if someone insults their God, and call for criminal pursuit of all blasphemers[16] but have no problem to call other Gods idols, demons or worse.

Then you shall know them by their fruits, i.e. by their works and actions, not their sayings or anything else (Matt 7:20). I deem that totally correct, however, I often notice that religious people like to worry more about the wrong faith and praise their sole right one than to judge the actual behaviour of those having an alleged wrong faith.

Finally, Jesus says the Sabbath was made for the people, not the other way round (Mark 2:27). He criticises the creation of bad situations by an overly pedantic observation of rituals, celebrations and other acts. In the Western culture nowadays you rarely meet people who refuse to switch on a light bulb in order to help someone in peril, but this statement has a broader sense. A ritual, a religious feast, the whole religion itself is made for man to give him a positive attitude and a basis in his life and not to force him to

[16] In Germany punished according to §166 StGB, but only when possibly violent masses disturbing the public peace can be found. Thus the more fundamentalist and violent a religious group is, the more drastic the country behaves against blasphemers mocking the faith of that group.

excel in performing rituals as exactly as possible. Of course, there are people who find strength in a well-defined normative framework, so this interpretation does not work for them. But to me it is in principle the same statement Cicero made by separating *superstitio* as excessive piety from the rightly performed *religio* (see page 16).

Although it is very interesting to analyse single aspects of a mythology in order to procure teachings for your own life and to learn whether the religion behind these myths suits you or not, the more important thing is the complete picture including its background. Religions contain a conception of man that determines how one should live in this world. In the previous chapter we discussed those parts of that conception that have a potential influence on a possible next life. Many religions state a human need for redemption, i.e. men is burden with bad karma, sins or bad behaviour by nature or by heritage from the first and original sinner or from a divine spark (– soul) fallen from the heavens. This separates men from the divine, the Gods or God, and man strives for redemption to be able to return there. That may be enabled by good deeds (e.g. Hinduism, Buddhism), by proper knowledge on the right way (e.g. gnosis with many varieties [Mar10]) or by a saviour whom you follow or have faith in – like Jesus in Christianity.

I dismiss the idea of redemption, especially the need of it. That idea is uncommon in Paganism, especially in the Germanic one. Here you work and live together with the Gods no matter what concept you have regarding them. "Together" is an important term here, you do not just work and live with them but together with them. There is no separation. They live in us, around us, among us or in our imagery. A redemption to return to them is therefore not necessary, neither in this world nor the next.

The only religion of redemption I know of and I find something positive about is the cult of Dionysus. Contrary to popular opinion this cult is not just about practising sexual, Lucullan and voluptuous feasts but is about rituals that help to ensure a proper afterlife. The followers of that cult believe that Dionysus grants them an afterlife in the Elysium which they perform in a religious ritual. That is very hedonistic but has a more serious background than the supposed simple pleasures. Also, the word "orgy" is still in use today but within this context in a very incorrect and defamatory way. It derives from the ancient Greek ὄργια = "sacred purpose" [Kla95], so in a figurative sense it means "divine service" or "sacrifice".

The following sentences are written on the epitaph of a Sabazios-priest (Sabazios is the Thracian-Phrygian variant of Dionysus). I like them very much and they can be well used for grace at meals or celebrations [Klo06]:

Manduca, bibe, lude et veni ad me
Cum vives, bene fac, hoc tecum feres.

Eat, drink, play, and come to me [, Sabazios/Dionysus]
As long as you live, enjoy yourself
This you will take with you [into the Elysium].

To shed some light on the fascinating details of the Nordic-Germanic Heathenism which fit to my attitude towards life, I would like to first look at some of the preserved scriptures first, and then at the Gods and some other mythological entities in general. Afterwards, at certain Gods individually and what is important to me about them, then at the virtues to be followed, and lastly the handling of destiny.

The most important writings to mention are the two Eddas; the Poetic or elder and the Prose or younger Edda. In addition we have Icelandic sagas, Skaldic poetry and Old-German texts. Of the latter only very few have survived. There is the Lay of Hildebrand (*Hildebrandslied*), whose pagan origin is not without doubt, and the Merseburg Charms (*Merseburger Zaubersprüche*) dealing with pagan Gods and other mythological beings. All these writings do not have as high of a significance within Paganism as scriptures do in the book or revealed religions. Its content and teachings may be regarded to be holy, but in a primary religion they do not constitute the religion, as is the case in a secondary one (on the distinction primary/secondary religion see page 22). Thus the designation "holy scripture" or "holy book" would be misleading.

Especially with the Prose Edda one has to keep in mind that its – possibly not sole – author Snorri Sturloson was a Christian scholar, whose intention for writing down pagan stories is not really known. It is regarded as a lesson on Skaldic poetry, maybe to preserve that form of literature and art. To understand and to compose verses utilising the stylistic devices "kenning" and "heiti" [Spa81], which both use mythical metaphors, it is vital to know the content of the cited myths and events. It is plausible that in a Christian environment such motivation allowed the writing down of pagan myths or was even necessary in the first place. It is not known if this was Snorri's true intention or just an excuse for the public to preserve Heathenism at least in writing. But many presume today that Snorri had an anthropological interest or even was a secret heathen.

Also related to this issue is Snorri's euhemeristic explanation in the Gylfaginning that the Gods were early human rulers coming from the city of Troy. Such a concept of the gods is based on the views of the Greek philosopher Euhemerus who stated that some of the deeds performed by famous ancestors were so outstanding that the ancestors themselves were honoured as Gods by their descendants [Doc01]. I do not accept that view. It is just a reversal of a bad habit often made by noble families in proclaiming themselves as descendants of the Gods. This inheritance is their basis of claim as rulers. A euhemeristic interpretation ascribes it to real circumstances instead of just showing-off. Troy is very popular for such a claim. The Roman family *gens Iulia* for example – a famous member was Gaius Iulius Caesar – also claimed to be descendants of Aeneas, the legendary hero, who escaped from Troy. Therefore names connected to that city appear quite often in heroic literature, e.g. the epithet of Hagen of Tronje in the *Nibelungenlied,* who is called "Hogni" in the Thidreks saga. Lord Raglan criticises this fabrication of pedigrees in his book [Rag03]. Fictitious ancestors are not necessarily gods but also often famous men from very old times. Lord Raglan gives examples of English pedigrees with impossible combinations like Norman names for alleged Saxon ancestors.

Snorri may have used this approach to publish pagan content without risking Christian censorship. The title Gylfaginning = "Tricking of Gylfi" alone implies, that the actual story was extended with elements that made it less suspicious in the Christian environment. This technique was quite common in medieval literature.

The Poetic Edda is closer to pagan origins but probably has some Christian influence too, which can be felt in some verses. This is not surprising, as Heathenism and Christianity coexisted peacefully in Scandinavia for quite some time. I regard the teachings, virtues and ethics portrayed in the Poetic Edda, especially in the Hávamál = „sayings of the High One", to be true and I did that long before I noticed their occurrence in the Germanic mythology.

Closely related to literature are the runes. They were not only used for various inscriptions, for profane and also higher reasons, they were often used in magic rites too, foretelling in particular. I have stated my views on magic in the relevant chapter and I certainly have nothing against using runology to gain something positive in life but regarding the effectiveness of predictions garnered from thrown runes, I stick to the aforementioned Hávamál [Poe12]:

> Certain is that which is sought from runes,
> That the Gods so great have made,
> And the Master-Poet painted;
> of the race of Gods:
> Silence is safest and best.

The Nordic-Germanic pantheon fits best to my personal views in two ways: First, there is the possibility to take the Gods as anthropomorphic ideals and natural forces; second, how to live my life, for which they epitomise on an ethical and moral scale or with regard to the attitudes towards life. The first part is more or less automatically the case with any other pagan pantheon, but the latter makes it necessary to take a more detailed look at the individual Gods and their attributes, i.e. in comparison to the Gods from different pantheons.

The distinction between the two divine lineages Æsir und Vanir, even though this might be an invention made purely by Snorri alone and most likely not by our heathen ancestors [Sim06b], is very close to my distinction between anthropomorphic ideals and natural forces, as the Æsir are roughly the Gods of culture and civilisation, namely the ideals, and the Vanir are more like natural forces. Of course, this distinction is not absolute, and a more stringent distinction would not be fitting. Their war is similar to the one between the Greek Gods, as the bringers of culture, and the Titans, as subordinate forces of nature, but it does not end in the total downfall of the Vanir. It ends with a reconciliatory peace and later cooperation. This can be interpreted as a symbiosis of the attachment to nature and of culture with all its possibilities to damage the environment such as irresponsible industrialisation. The destruction of the environment by man-made culture is not a phenomenon of modern times, as many might believe: The people in the Palaeolithic Age already lived in a throwaway society with extensive garbage dumps, as excavated Stone Age settlements in Britannia and Scandinavia prove, e.g. Skara Brae on the Scottish island Orkney.

The individual Germanic Gods do not have such precisely defined "fields of duty" as the Greek ones. This has pros and cons. The Germanic pantheon is clearly more complicated than the Greek one, not because of the sheer number of gods and other mythological beings, which is far smaller simply due to the lacking sources, but through the split and assignment of "tasks" and "responsibilities". This makes the answer to the question, what God shall be called for what reason in a ritual, a bit more complicated and by no means conclusive. But it allows calling for the same God under different aspects, which is also possible in the Greek mythology but not that pronounced.

I would now like to take a closer look at some of the Gods. I will limit myself to the aspects that are important for the explanation of my attitude towards Nordic-Germanic Heathenism, although this leaves out some Gods who are very important to me in other respects like Víðarr and Ullr, just to name a few. For a detailed and comprehensive description of all the Gods and their attributes, particularities and interpretations please refer to the proper specialist literature. A spiritual insight into such divine aspects cannot be gathered from books anyway, for that I recommend ritual practice and a deliberate engagement with the according mythology itself.

At first there is Odin, who is commonly called the highest, leader or king of the Gods. I do not agree with those hierarchical titles and believe they are rather based on the change from Heathenism to Christianity, which changed the structure of sovereignty as well, than on the mythological texts. Odin does not give orders to anybody in the myths, neither to men nor to other Gods. If he intervenes or steers, then by notes, discussions, and metaphorical or open speech, which befits his role as the God of knowledge and wisdom and the acquisition of both. He leads others by giving them insights into correct behaviours, not by giving commands and expecting obedience.

Furthermore the Gods always meet in council before making important and essential decisions. Therefore I see Odin more as a council leader than a ′king in a divine court among tributary subjects. If the Gods are regarded as something which brings order into the worldly chaos, namely something like a government or administration, then we have democratic structures here. Likewise the Germanic Thing was a grass-roots affair, though you have to be extremely careful with those modern terms coming from completely different cultural conditions. We even have some kind of separation of powers here. Odin can be regarded as a member of the legislative, Thor as a member of the executive and Forseti as an allegory of the judiciary. The latter was elected by the Gods even to judge them, a more democratic system is hardly possible. Tyr as the Heavenly Father (see page 51) is something like a grey eminence in the background, quite comparable to the German president. In summary we see that there is no supreme ruler or highest god in the Germanic pantheon. The Greek pantheon is a bit more monarchistic with its mightiest god as a ruler. Personally I identify Odin more with Apollon than with Zeus. Both are ideals for science, especially for medicine and healing, which is described in the 2nd Merseburg Incantation on Odin/Wodan's part. Even if you regard Odin as a ruler rather than a chairman legitimised by society, the highest god in the Germanic pantheon is not the mightiest but the wisest. This may sound surprising: Thor counts as the most powerful God, often called "the strongest", and Víðarr as second. In that list of pure power Odin comes on place three at the earliest, while I do perceive of one or two other Gods before him. It is his mind and knowledge which brought him to the top not sheer force or means from his arsenal. That is something to think about.

It is assumed that Odin was adored by the upcoming noble gentry, while the lower classes worshipped Thor at the top of the list. This would fit with the ruler aspect of Odin. Thor however is regarded as the friend of mankind who protects the world form all kinds of harm. This protection is symbolised in the struggles against various mythological creatures such as Jörmungandr, the Midgard Serpent, or giants.

This protection does not work perfectly, due to the simple fact that the pagan Gods are not omnipotent, including the highest one. Therefore something may happen through destiny which was not intended or wanted by them or even was against their explicit will. Due to that circumstance the theodicy-problem cannot appear in pagan religion, as it automatically does in Christianity. When you compare the concept of benevolent and almighty gods with the real state of this world, it cannot be explained by free will or sinful actions alone. Natural disasters such as tsunamis, that kill hundreds of thousands, do occur by different means and without any human intervention or failure. As we have already seen, a literal although maybe naïve omnipotence is mathematically impossible anyway (see page 56).

One aspect of Thor is his violent temper, which to my knowledge is in no myth directed against people but always against things threatening the world of men. In the legend of Thjalfi and Röskva, Loki appeased his anger. In the Hárbarðsljóð he receives a setback from Odin disguised as a ferryman, who does not let him pass a river despite all his anger and threats. Now, a river is certainly not an insurmountable obstacle to a God usually riding a flying chariot. Instead, the tale demonstrates that even the strongest and mightiest God has limits, and how Odin actually gives his council.

The by far mostly misunderstood God is Loki. The common public usually regards him as the Germanic variant of Satan, thus the spawn of evil and in permanent opposition to the Gods. In fact, he has a very ambivalent character in the myths. Asgard would not have been built without him, Thor would not have gotten back his stolen hammer, and he is the blood brother of Odin. Some identify him with Lóðurr, who creates the first human couple together with Odin and Hœnir, because the triad Odin, Hœnir and Loki appears in the Faroese ballad Loka Táttur. Besides those positive aspects he tricks the blind Höðr into killing his brother Baldr and at Ragnarok he fights on the side of those who want to destroy the world.

You can see this ambivalence in his descendants too. He gives birth to Sleipnir[17], Hel, the Midgard Serpent and the Fenris Wolf. Sleipnir as Odin's riding horse can be seen as something very positive, Hel as the Goddess of Death with her beautiful and ugly side has an ambivalent character too, and the latter two are clearly something negative as they are threatening the basis of this world. Thus Loki is not regarded as someone intrinsically evil but as someone whose actions are necessary but also very dangerous.

There are many things in this world which are necessary and dangerous. A good example with a mythical background is fire. There are three mythological beings in close relation to fire who symbolise different aspects and meanings of it. Baldr as a Sun-God can be seen as a source of warmth and light, which he gives to the people. Thus, he embodies the pure positive aspect of fire.

Loki symbolises the fire which is necessary but dangerous for people, for example a stove fire. You need it to prepare food but it can destroy your house if you are not careful. The Norwegians utter phrases like "Lokje beats his children", when the hearth fire crackles. Leftovers thrown into the fire are "for Lokje" [Sim06b]. An extreme and very modern example of such a "fire" is the nuclear one. Nuclear power is the most effective and rich energy source yet available, but woe to us if a major accident happens. Also you must

[17]Sleipnir is always depicted with eight legs on ancient images. There are different views about the reason, from a symbol for four pallbearers, because Odin rode to the neither world on Sleipnir to the comic-like illustration of speed. I find the latter quite interesting, as it showed that our ancestors' feeling for art might have been surprisingly close to ours today.

deal very carefully and cautiously with its “descendants”, the radioactive waste.

Surtr is the fire giant and guardian of Muspelheim who will one day start the conflagration that destroys the world. He stands for devastating fire without any sense or need. An Ekpyrosis, the end of the world in a great fire, is found in many mythologies. From a purely scientific viewpoint, this is exactly going to happen one day when the Sun turns into a red giant and will either destroy the Earth or at least make it uninhabitable [Sag82].

We have already talked about Tyr’s role as a Heavenly Father which is missing in the Eddas, but his limited role as a God of War therein contains two lessons that I could not find in other war-gods like Ares/Mars in such an expressive form. When the Gods want to tame the Fenris Wolf, Tyr deceives him and must sacrifice his right hand in a deceit to restrain him. This is necessary to protect the world. If you understand the story to be a symbol of warfare, you can see a demand and a warning regarding war. Here, war is not intended to be an aggressive gain of power or riches but is for defending something valuable against a serious threat. Furthermore, it will demand irretrievable sacrifices. Even a God loses his sword hand, which illustrates the horrors and deplorable losses among countrymen, friends and relatives caused by the war.

In the Nordic-Germanic paganism the so-called “Nine Noble Virtues ” are often presented as an ethical and moral concept. This collection of virtues, taken from the myths, is a very recent one and cannot be found in older literature or even in the myths themselves in that particular form. The number 9 itself has a figurative meaning. It is an allusion to the nine mythical worlds and the square number of 3, another number playing a great role in religious circles, e.g. divine triads or the Trinity[18]. This specific count of virtues alone

[18] I always asked myself why the number 3 is so prominent in so many religions and beliefs. My answer is that it is the very first number which goes beyond the purely human. Humans have one or two similar body parts (apart from fingers and toes which still occur in pairs, and the many hairs) and two genders.

imply that we do not have an exact account of something to follow or obey here. Overlaps and omissions are possible.

Depending on the group which has written them down the individual virtues are sometimes a bit different but usually very similar. They are:

- courage or bravery
- truth or honesty
- honour
- loyalty or fidelity
- discipline or self-control
- hospitality
- diligence or industriousness
- independence, self-confidence or self-reliance
- perseverance, endurance or steadfastness

You can observe some overlap here. Disciple and diligence together can make up steadfastness. Self-reliance without discipline might be rather difficult to obtain. Some virtues are missing here, but with a little imagination you can subsume them under the existing ones. Punctuality for example is a part of discipline. Education is a mix of truth, self-reliance and a bit of endurance. Law-abiding behaviour can be seen as a form of loyalty.

These virtues are not a well-defined standard of conduct. Which actions are appropriate depends on the situation. As an ethical principle I think it is better to consider the implications in each individual case and based on that consideration decide individually how to act rather than follow a dogmatic set of norms without any alternatives.

Some formulate the virtues in the pattern "X is better than its opposite". Courage turns into "courage is better than cowardice", truth into "truth is better than a lie". This pattern displays a basic policy to be followed whenever possible, but also allows permissible deviations from that principle in limited cases when necessary. We all know situations in which a white lie keeps the peace between people far better than the genuine truth. The greatest courage is useless against severe dangers when you lack the necessary resources to fight them effectively. A cowardly escape can save your live and provide opportunities for future and possible actions. All this may sound terribly trivial, but if you take a look at the radical methods of not only religious but also political fundamentalist groups, which follow ideologies lacking those exceptions and alternatives, you recognise the importance of this ethical principle. This does not mean the habitual ignorance of values and norms, as in the exploitation of almost any situation without ethical or moral constraints, but about a rational and commonly acceptable basis to follow in general but not necessarily at any cost.

A simple, reasonable and practicable maxim is the "Golden Rule" that states, you should treat others as you would like to be treated by them [Höf08]. The Wiccan Read formulates that as "do whatever you like as long as you are not hurting anyone else with it" [Wik12d].

In Germanic Heathenism your individual behaviour depends strongly on the actions of your counterparts. This follows the principle of mutuality, which is also expressed symbolically in the sacrificial practices (see page 73). To phrase it more simply: You treat your friends in a noticeably different way than your enemies, not only practically or when compelled but also in your mind and attitudes. This is the diametrical opposite of the Christian "love thy enemy" (Luke 6:27-36). You are not obliged to treat people, who deliberately try to harm you, like your nice neighbour. You may and are allowed to defend yourself with suitable means, including the disregard of certain virtues like the truth. You can misinform your enemies for tactical and strategic reason. To quote the Hávamál [Poe12]: "And fraud with falsehood meet."

This does not mean, that you should look for enemies or make some new ones, as many suppose who believe Germanic paganism was some kind of warriors' cult. In fact, the already cited Hávamál warns explicitly against such an attitude:

> The man who is prudent, a measured use
> Of the might he has will make;
> He finds when among the brave he fares
> That the boldest he may not be.

It is rather a way to cope with one's imposed fate and to fight against that if necessary. (More on that later.) It is not an "eye for an eye, a tooth for a tooth" strategy, but rather the permission and also the duty to defend yourself and to act against threats and dangers. Something, which is regulated by our modern law for the very same purpose by the way.

The mutuality and exceptions from a dogmatic norm are especially important in the case of loyalty. Loyalty is not a one-way street but a bilateral relationship. Whoever enters a contract, promises something, swears an oath or commits to something by any means must of course comply with his vows. And of course the other side has to do the very same thing. But as soon as the other side breaks such a relationship deliberately, your own obligation vanishes, especially if the other side acted with malicious intent. Our established common laws and practices regarding purchase, labour or other agreements consider all that too. But it is quite different when it comes to hierarchical or spiritual relations.

The loyalty to a sovereign, a God or a philosophical principle is usually rated higher than the return to be expected and therefore often called for without any loyalty or compensation from the other side. Now, it is very difficult to measure the return of a principle, and you can argue on the possibilities to determine the gifts of a God. But it is relatively easy to see whether there is a bilateral relationship between human rulers and subordinates or only obedience from down below and grace from above. And it does not matter here if we talk about monarchs, a ruling class or caste, a powerful organisation or democratically legitimised hierarchies.

The virtue of honour needs a closer examination because it is easily misunderstood and is often associated with quite inappropriate dealings, such as honour killings which happen in fundamentalist religious environments. The term "honour" has roughly two meanings. At first people can receive honours from others for their own successful deeds. Maybe a better word here is „glory". The virtuous behaviour then is to perform glorious deeds and to praise others for their honourable actions. That is certainly nothing wrong but it seems a bit banal to me. This interpretation of honour has only then a deeper meaning if you consider fame and glory as necessary for your own legacy when you have left the world, as the Hávamál might indicate, see page 98.

Personally, I rather see honour as something you keep as long as you act honourably, i.e. complying with your own values and ethics. Or like a German colloquialism says, as long as you are able to endure your own face in a mirror. You lose honour by dishonourable actions, i.e. those which do not comply with their own ethics while taking into account the above-mentioned possible exceptional situations. From this perspective, it is actually an error in terms of category to put honour into a list of virtues, as it describes how to deal with your virtues instead of being one itself. It is important with this viewpoint that nobody can give you honour or take away your honour; it is all up to you. Dishonourable behaviour, which roughly corresponds to "sin" in Christianity, cannot be forgiven. You have to amend the damage that was produced by your dishonourable actions. Compare this interpretation of honour with the legend of Thjalfi and Röskva, page 34.

To me a very crucial issue with Nordic-Germanic paganism is its view on destiny; how to handle it and how the Gods are involved in it.

The past produces the framework for our current actions. It forces us to certain decisions and actions, while other, greater and uncontrollable things simply happen. The present determines the future in the very same way the past does for the present. Your own current decisions and deeds directly shape a part of the whole future, whereby each and every event and action is connected to everything else in the world.

This mixture of decisions, based on free will affecting the future and of circumstances or inevitable events forced upon us, makes up a world-view that in my judgement fits far better with reality than many of the others. The possibilities for people to decide and act by their free will are limited, however, there is no strict determinism that prevents any human influence on the future, and otherwise, free will would be determined as well. Thus you do not fall into fatalism when you accept an inevitable fate, as you still know about the theoretical possibility to change it, as limited as it may though be.

The Nordic-Germanic mythology illustrates that beautifully. The cosmic interconnections are represented in the web of destiny woven by the Norns Urðr, Verðandi and Skuld. The Norns correlate (in that very order) with the past, the present and the future, and their Old Norse names etymologically shed some light on the world-view regarding fate. Urðr means "destiny" or roughly "was", "has become to" (*urðum*), Verðandi "to be", "to become" (*werden* in German) and Skuld ("which needs to be") has connections to the German word *Schuld* which means "debt", "liability", "obligation" or "guilt" [Sim06b].

The German prefix *ur-* also denotes something very old or past, which is the basis for something present: *Uralt* ("age-old"), *Urzeit* ("primeval times"), *Ursprung* ("origin", "source"), *Ursache* ("cause"). An etymological relation is likely.

(The following paragraph has lost a lot in translation, therefore let me give some explanation of its original meaning and purpose: The German adjective *schuldig* (from *Schuld*) means "guilty", "responsible" or "being in debt" and always has a negative connotation in modern German. The adjective for "responsible" or "obliged" in a positive, negative or neutral way is *verantwortlich*. Therefore, the German original emphasises the neutral aspect of *Schuld* and how it is represented by Skuld.) Obligation is closely linked to the future here and bears no biased implications. The attribute "guilty" is generally a malicious or criminal act. You are guilty and responsible of the negative consequences caused by your actions. In the web of destiny this responsibility has a neutral meaning. You are responsible for any consequence your actions are causing. It can yield to something good and to fame or to something bad and damaging that needs to be repaired by you (see above regarding the virtue Honour).

An outstanding feature of the Nordic-Germanic Gods is that they are subject to fate too, just like humans. This applies to other pagan pantheons as well, e.g. Zeus and Sarpedon (page 20), but in the Greek mythology humans are much more the toys of the Gods who determine their destiny than in the Nordic-Germanic one. Here the Gods act within the web of destiny and the consequences of their actions result from the cause-action-responsibility principle of said web and it is not the Gods' sheer will that directly rules everything happening. This is linked to the lacking omnipotence and omniscience of heathen gods. Like us humans they can neither act outside the framework set by the past nor prevent the direct future consequences of their current actions.

My favourite mythological image is that every entity in this cosmos is caught in the web of destiny and is pulling its strings. Therefore everyone is influencing each other by his or her actions. Some pull weakly, some pull strongly, the Gods may pull extremely strong, but the overall end result of all this pulling is not determined by the will of some higher beings or one highest being alone. It is a holistic result of the whole network.

Men and Gods are sitting in one boat, they form a community of common fate by trying together to produce something positive and fight against the negative forces to prevent them. Those negative forces are personified by giants[19] or creatures like the Midgard Serpent and the Fenris Wolf, who are caught in the web as well and are combated by the Gods in the myths. I think this image is far more appropriate for free men than those in which a god or several gods dominate men by overwhelming power, dictate their lives and threaten them with harsh punishments if they do not comply to their wishes.

This collaborative relationship between humans and Gods is quite different from one between a supreme monarch and his minions or an instance, which declares the laws of nature surrounding us but is not subject to them itself, and those who are constrained by those laws. I believe this type of community makes a closer personal relationship to the Gods more possible than abstract theological concepts, even though those anthropomorphic images of the Gods are purely mythological and not ostensibly historical or real in a straight and literal way.

Human doubts about the Gods or disagreements among them are located on a different level too. A close fellowship that faces a common fate, works on the same accomplishments and tries to

[19] It must be noted that not every giant is a negative power fighting against Gods and humans. There are neutral and allied giants.

prevent a common menace, allows for meaningful criticism and some challenges between its members. That has nothing to do with a lack of respect but is an inherent property of such a community. A man may have problems with one or more Gods and may also mention them without automatically disturbing their relationship, which is not just based on a hierarchy but on common circumstances and shared destiny.

I once had a discussion with a philologist, whether Achilles' criticism of Apollo in the Iliad [Hom09] was a sign of his disrespect towards that God. Achilles complains that Apollo is fighting on the Trojan side and is denying him his glory. He announces that he would have his revenge on the God if he had enough power for such an accomplishment. I do not think that this is a lack of respect. Achilles does recognise Apollo's grandeur and divinity, he just does not feel well standing on the other side of the frontline or that the God is supporting the "wrong" side respectively. Here also the circumstances produced by fate cause the opposition, and not an apostasy or lack of faith.

As already mentioned on page 19, the myth of Ragnarok, the end of the world, can be interpreted in a way that it reflects the above said dealing with destiny. The end of the world and Odin's death are inevitable, but he arms and prepares himself against that fate, despite better knowledge. That is a very good role model for us, whose life will surely end one day and who must endure a terrible and inevitable fate from time to time. Your life and destiny can only be improved if you pull the web's strings woven by the Norns as strongly as you can instead of always being pulled by others.

Closely connected to fate is *hamingja*, an Old Norse term a bit difficult to translate. In Old Norse Heathenism it described the personified luck of a person, as a more abstract concept like "well-being" as well as a spiritual entity following that person. Such an entity was called *fylgja*.

In modern Heathenism hamingja is also a word for the luck of a group like the family, the kindred or a clan. After your own death your personal hamingja may pass to the group you formerly belonged to. There are parallels to the *karma* in Indian and East

Asian religions, though you usually take your karma into your next life instead of transferring it to your family.

Many consider hamingja as some kind of wealth you can win or lose and collect on an account. This account represents how well or bad your being is or might develop. With the web of destiny this makes sense, as we cannot completely control most of which is happening around us. The actions of others have a strong influence, which can be good or bad and will affect the future, thus there is always a certain potential for good and bad future conditions that comes from within us and from the outside world at the same time.

The common and modern German translation of hamingja is *Heil*, which derives from the Old and Middle High German *heil* = "luck". Further meanings are "health" (*heilen* = "to heal"), "wholeness" ("whole" has obviously a strong etymological connection to *Heil*) and, in a religious context, "salvation". As a greeting phrase ("hail"), which today is no longer politically correct, it expresses the wish, that the greeted may gain health or happiness. The Old English word *hael* means "omen of good fortune".

Hamingja has a second meaning, the modified form of someone who is able to transform his shape [Sim06b]. Shape shifting and fortune are often connected in songs and myths – for obvious reasons, as luck is constantly changing. This is nicely illustrated in the best-known song of the Carmina Burana, which calls the Goddess of Fortune in its very first line [Car95]:

O Fortuna
velut luna, statu variablis
semper crescis, aut decrescis

O Fortune,
like the moon, you are changeable
ever waxing, and waning

To me a very important issue in paganism is that there is no ideological dualism. There is no strict division between an absolute good and an absolute evil people that have to use for orientation. While humans are in a position somewhere in-between those extremes, religions provide ways to get closer to the good position – by divine grace or rigid moral norms. This dualism lives on in the notions of an afterlife with one absolutely heavenly and one absolute hellish place. Sometimes the dead end up between those extreme positions somewhere, e.g. the purgatory (see page 100), before their final destination is decided.

Such a good-evil dualism with its corresponding personalisation like God and Satan is often found in monotheistic religions, even though in the myths the good god usually has more power than the evil side. For example in Zoroastrianism, the Persian religion of Zoroaster, who created some spiritual basics which were later adopted by the Abrahamitic monotheisms, the good and evil side have exactly the same power, which is necessary for a strict dualism. The Avesta Yasna, one of the Zoroastrian holy scriptures, tells about the pair Ahura Mazda and Ahriman [Wol10]: "A vision has revealed as a pair of twins, two spirits at the beginning, who are the good and evil in thought, word, and deed; and between both of them those who are understanding and the ignorant have made the right choice."

However, the entities of pagan mythology are ambivalent. They do not represent the absolute and dualistic good and evil but more detailed aspects. Although there are higher and lower beings – in the Nordic-Germanic context the "High Ones", namely the Gods, and the "beings of nether mythology" including anyone else – but that is not a distinction between good and evil. As already mentioned, even Loki, who is often falsely seen as the Germanic devil, is not an absolute evil in a dualistic sense. However, there are many discussions among heathens, whether he is actually a God or a giant, a said being of nether mythology. I treat this question as a matter of personal assessment and thus relationship. He is a God to those who offer him sacrifices or worship him.

The thoughts and actions of the mythological beings is neither good nor evil but directed by their ideals. If religious people gain something positive or negative from those thoughts and actions, it depends on the circumstances, the destiny and their perception. Someone following those ideals has to consider the consequences, the responsibility for the future (see above) and right or wrong behaviour, but there is no fundamental and absolute connection to good or bad polar opposites. Almost no one on this world hurts someone else out of pure wickedness. Everyone acts out of necessity or supposedly good intentions and objectives. That does not mean you are not entitled to fight those who try to hurt you. On the contrary, Nordic-Germanic heathenism allows and encourages you to fight back, it just does not propagate the nimbus of the opponent or enemy acting only from dreadful evilness.

Readers with knowledge of modern paganism might have noticed that I have avoided some established terms so far. This was done with full intent to coherently deliver the essentials of my philosophy behind heathenism first, before potentially biased terms could produce distractive or false impressions.

Modern Nordic-Germanic Heathenism is usually called "Asatru". This word is derived from the Icelandic *ásatrú* = "faith in the Æsir". The syllable "tru" is etymologically related to "truth", "trust", and the German *Treue* = "loyalty". Personally I prefer the German term *Asentreue* ("loyalty to the Æsir") over Asatru, simply because of the onomatopoeic similarity. Furthermore trust and loyalty fit better to my views than faith or belief, and regarding my god-conceptions, it roughly means the same anyway. Unfortunately this internationally common word is politically charged a bit due to its usage in certain circles. Although there is no general basis for this political bias, as we will see in detail in the appendix, I did not want to raise any premature prejudices.

There are two movements within Asatru which can be identified, "folkish" and "universalist", especially in the United States. In Germany, the term *völkisch* (translation for "folkish") almost automatically creates an impression of racism and exaggerated nationalism due to historical circumstances. In fact, "folkish" does not necessarily mean racism but the concept that the religion is fundamentally based on the folk, i.e. the ethnicity, and the according culture [Gol05a]. Members of other ethnic groups or cultures are not to be discriminated or even persecuted, they are only regarded to be unsuitable or unable to participate or join. Of course the border between cultural ethnocentrism and racist or nationalistic extremism is hard to find [Kel98]. Many may have already crossed that border, but to deduce that all folkish people are racists is simply wrong.

Universalists do not practice a sealing-off against other races or cultures, but many of them think that members of the indigenous culture have a far easier access to Asatru than those from other cultures. I think that this notion is totally right. You can test how hard it is to understand religions from other cultures by trying to grasp Buddhism, Taoism or Shintoism. This is anything but easy, because you simply do not know the cultural characteristics and philosophies that are part of those religions or even its very basis. The average Western world citizen already fails in understanding modern and ancient paganism, to expect or even demand this from foreigners coming from distant countries is illusory. Of course, some greater difficulties in cultural communication is no reason to exclude someone honestly interested from participation, such as is quickly or usually done in ethnocentrism.

Modern pagans are few and many of them do not want to organise, thus compiling statistics is rather difficult. In Germany roughly 500 Nordic-Germanic heathens are organised in associations. On the internet you notice a bigger interest but to count reliable numbers here is almost impossible. Two years ago I estimated about 2,000 – 3,000, not more than 5,000 religiously active Nordic-Germanic pagans in Germany, but today, after a lot of unplanned and unforeseen contacts and meetings I'd say we are a lot more. Maybe 10,000, which is 0.012% of the total population over here and statistically insignificant in all respects.

The worldwide situation is not much different. Even in Iceland, where in 1972 the founding of the association Íslenska Ásatrúarfélagið re-established the Nordic paganism in the modern Western world, member numbers are modest although in relative relations far greater compared to other countries. Ásatrúarfélagið has roughly 1,500 members, which is nearly 0.5% of the total population. The founder Sveinbjörn Beinteinsson did get the official recognition as a religious denomination in 1973 though. Anyway, low membership rates should not discourage us to follow and practice what we honour and venerate.

Within Asatru, there are different approaches how to practice the religion. These differences do not regard how rituals are celebrated or on which date certain feasts are held but how the religion in general is accepted or lived. Combinations of those alignments are possible of course. There are people who perform magic and neo-shamanic practices. Others are engaged in scientific, mainly historical and archaeological exercises, particularly regarding the myths and sagas. Of course, this is a widespread common procedure. Attempting to reconstruct the ancient rites as accurately as possible is closely connected to the historical research.

Sometimes, especially in Germany, a distinction between neopaganism and old or original paganism is made. It is of course formally correct that modern paganism is different than the past and former. So much was forgotten and destroyed by the invading monotheism that a great part of contemporary paganism must be reinvented. The efforts to precisely reconstruct rituals and festival are worthy but not sufficient for practical use due to the inadequate amount of historical sources.

A steady and constant development from the old to contemporary Heathenism is not given due to the total disruption in the early to late middle ages. A new start to some extent is thus necessary. I still regard the term neopaganism to be a little misguided. The earth keeps revolving, times keep changing – and most heathens are aware of that. The indigenous pagan religion would have changed anyway, especially if people were open to cultural and scientific progress. And anyone honouring Odin as the ideal for acquiring and maintaining knowledge and wisdom should have an open mind towards science, research and progress.

Therefore, I see no essential difference between the older and modern paganism with the exception of the inevitable amendments by progress and zeitgeist. I treat the terms neopaganism and old paganism like modern and Old English, which describe the same language in different ages.

In this respect, all contemporary pagans are neopagans, which makes the term trivial. It is like calling contemporary English "Neoenglish" all the time. However, there are some who believe or pretend to follow or practice the only valid and exactly defined original Heathenism of our ancestors and not some distinguishable neopaganism. That I regard as impossible – solely because of the above said lack of proper historical sources. It might be possible, with some limitations, for ancient cults known from the Roman Empire but not for the Nordic-Germanic religion. But no matter, I consider the possibility to follow the same religion on different paths as something positive.

For today's paganism which acknowledges the scientific, cultural progress of civilization over the last few centuries, especially that made during the Age of Enlightenment and integrates that progress into its views and ideas, I argue for the name:

Enlightened Heathenism.

(This is the direct translation of the book's original title "Aufgeklärtes Heidentum" and might be a little misleading. "Enlightened" has two different meanings in English, in German there are two separate words, *erleuchtet* = "enlightened (in a spiritual sense)" and *aufgeklärt* = "enlightened (historical, philosophical)". This translation refers to the latter and the historical Age of Enlightenment.)

That nicely summarises the virtues of old traditions and new findings. The Enlightenment has brought us human and civil rights or at least has tried to do so, although in many places today we do not see much of them. Its motto is *sapere aude!* = "Dare to be reasonable!" or "Have the courage to use your own mind!", which is known by Immanuel Kant [Kan84] but originates in the Epistles of Horaz[20]. I think it is very suitable for a modern and open-minded religion to set it apart from old-fashioned and outdated dogmas.

The creation of a truly enlightened and liberal society, has not happened yet. A society in which everyone can be religious according to their own ideas as long as no harm comes to others. Religion in general is still seen as a dogmatic system of absolute

---

[20] The unabridged original is: *Dimidium facti, qui coepit, habet: sapere aude, incipe!* = "Halfway has finished, who has started: Dare to be wise, now begin!" (Epistula I,2,40) [Fla00].

faith. Paganism, and I do hope in particular the modern one, shows that this is not the only religious way. A pagan understanding of religion inherently provides many different paths to walk on instead of a single one.

In my opinion natural science in particular is not a mutually exclusive but a parallel path to the religious one, see page 20. This attitude does not only apply to paganism alone. Many other religious people think the same way but the basic concepts within paganism make it easier to mix science and religion then many other beliefs, as I have tried to explain in this book. It is a serious and immense error to treat the lessons of life told in the myths as physical or biological theories, whether because the latter are still undiscovered, not understood or not accepted. That includes the functional development of the cosmos, life and consciousness. To find the meaning of life within the cosmos is better situated in the area of religion rather than of science.

There is a story from the last days of ancient Graeco-Roman paganism, which, among other things, tells us about those many ways and contains a cry for freedom of religion. That cry has completely vanished shortly thereafter for one and a half millennia from the political structures in Europe.

Christianity stood on the brink to become the state religion. In the Senate of Rome an altar of the Goddess Victoria, the Altar of Victory, was erected for so long that the Christians wanted to have it removed. From now on there should not be any symbol of the old state religion in public facilities. This reminds us of present atheistic campaigns to have Christian crosses removed from classrooms, courtrooms and other public places because it is the symbol of the current de facto but outdated state religion. In late ancient times the pagans fought for the Altar of Victory; today Christians want to save their crosses in public institutions and are thus fighting exactly the same thing that their predecessors did in the 4th century. Quintus Aurelius Symmachus, one of the last defenders of ancient heathenism, wrote the following words in a letter to Emperor Flavius Valentinianus, also known as Valentinian II., which still should be listened to today. It is proof that even in ancient times different paths to the same target were seen as something positive [Sym73]:

We ask, then, for peace for the Gods of our fathers and of our country.
It is just that all worship should be considered as one.
We look on the same stars, the sky is common, the same world surrounds us.
What difference does it make by what pains each seeks the truth?
We cannot attain to so great a secret by one road.

APPENDIX – RIGHT-WING EXTREMISM AND 3RD REICH

A common prejudice and accusation is that being a Germanic pagan also means being a right-winged extremist. This assumption is based on the perception of philosophical and political currents in the 19th and 20th century which assimilated and used pagan symbols and texts. The public is not really aware of modern Heathenism and its ideas and notions simply because of its tiny scale. Therefore it is frequently confused or equated with much better known esoteric views.

Of course, there were and still are radical right-wing heathens, just as there are right-wing Christians, Muslims or Jews, even though the latter are certainly not anti-Semitic. A serious logical fallacy is to conclude from this that all members of a religion must have the very same orientation. Even if the religion is followed by some with extreme political views.

Germanic Heathenism is almost always associated with nationalistic or racist ideology, sometimes it is even portrayed as the philosophy behind the Third Reich and the central idea within National Socialist society. Along with the previously mentioned 19th century occultism, it shares this fate with Satanism and atheism, which both are often said to be the hidden agenda behind the National Socialist movement. Instead, I say this is propaganda spread by those who philosophically or theologically disagree with all these views. It has nothing to do with reality.

I intend to show here that this alleged connection between paganism and the Third Reich is a historical coincidence. Paganism is not the philosophical or ideological foundation of that political movement. Furthermore, any real influence of paganism on the Third Reich has been analysed and clearly shows that that state was far less heathen than many suppose or pretend. Even despite some prominent esoterics who had a soft spot for neopaganism.

The rediscovery of the Germanic myths and their cultural and artistic treatment happened in the 19th century. At that time and in the early 20th century a lot of esoteric and occult circles were created which unscrupulously utilised the rediscovered symbols and texts but did not connect to heathen traditions and did not want or dare to reconstruct the ancient religions as such. Some of those ideas and philosophies became quite popular, their founders were or even still are celebrities. Anthroposophy by Rudolf Steiner, Ariosophy by Guido von List, Theosophy by Helena Blavatski, Theozoology by Jörg Lanz von Liebenfels etc. etc., the list is long. At the very same time an exaggerated nationalism and racism occurred as well, which proposed a society consisting only of people belonging to a single ethnic group. A mutual influence and some connections are thus likely.

After World War I, the so-called Thule society began its political activities and started to spread anti-Semitic propaganda [His12b]. It was a trailblazer of National Socialism but completely lost its importance in the 1930s. Its founder, Rudolf von Sebottendorf[21] had close connections to the occult and racist Ariosophy by von List, which is the basis of many conspiracy theories and wild speculations about the occult origins of the National Socialist movement [Car06]. The Thule society had only 200 members at the beginning and was dissolved as early as 1925. Von Sebottendorf was deported from Germany, when he attempted to reactivate it in 1934 [Goo00].

This example of the rather famous Thule society indicates that the actual influence of the early occult and esoteric circles on the later established Third Reich was low to non-existent. The opposite impression is created by the excessive and partially inappropriate usage of its symbolism and not by the real adherence to the philosophical content of those movements.

It was already addressed in the former chapter that ethnocentrism plays a major role in some parts of contemporary Nordic-Germanic Heathenism. This folkish idea is often confused with racism, which cannot have any basis in the religious mythology, as the racist ideology itself emerged centuries after the myths were written down.

The English spa Bath is a good example of how religion and other public affairs were handled in ancient times without any ethnic or cultural distinction. The story is nicely illustrated in the local "Roman Baths" museum [Rom12].

---

[21] Offical name: Rudolf Glauer [His12b].

There was a hot spring the Celtic locals had consecrated to the Goddess of the Sun and Healing, Sulis. The Romans identified her as Minerva using their *interpretatio Romana* and built a temple dedicated to Minerva-Sulis directly at the spring along with a public bath, hence the town's name. Thus the worship of Sulis could continue unabated under Roman rule. The religious surroundings have changed a bit but were not completely replaced as it would have happened if certain other forms of religion had taken over. To put it into modern language; here we see an effective integration policy being applied.

(The following paragraph was originally about the German word *Volk* = "folk", "nation", "ethnic group", but I guess the etymology of "folk" is identical. In German the term *Volk* often has a racist connotation, hence this explanation about its original meaning.) The term "folk" is a combination of the Proto-Indo-European root for "full" (*voll*) and "many" (*viele*), as well as the old Slavic *plŭkŭ* = "armed band", hence the word *Pulk* (German for "group of people", related to the English word "bulk") [Gri12]. Thus "*Volk*/folk" only meant "many people" or "armed band" before the modern era. An ethnic connotation especially in an ideological sense did not yet exist in former times.

To directly infer an ethnocentrism or racism from the heathen mythology is not possible. The loose connection of these forms of religion and ideology is a historical coincidence from the 19th century. However, there are some who conclude the concept of racial segregation from the story told in the Rígsmál. Ríg, another name for Heimdallr, fathers the three classes of people, i.e. servants, free men and nobles. The first progenitors of those classes were called Þræll, Karl and Jarl [Sim76]. *Jarl* is a Nordic noble title and related to the English *Earl*. The Rígsmál is clearly an etiology, i.e. a mythical narrative, about the construction of the current social order back then. To regard it as the basis of a racial ideology or for the practice of racial segregation requires the interpretation of the classes as races and cannot be taken directly from the content.

By the way, you can find a similar interpretation in biblical myths [Lew82]. In the story of the Flood Noah is the progenitor of all modern humans There are his three sons – Shem, Ham and

Japheth – "of them was the whole earth overspread" (Gen 9:19). Racial segregation and racial discrimination is explained and justified with the cursing of Ham and all his descendants by Noah (Gen 9:25-27). The experts deny that this could be the original intention of this myth. The curse does not hit a race but the geographical region [22] Canaan and is connected to the biblical Israelite conquest of Canaan [Gol05b].

When regarding right-wing extremism, anti-Judaism is interesting as it differs from anti-Semitism through the absence of the racist component. Like other racist ideas, anti-Semitism grew in the 19th century, while anti-Judaism was almost always an inherent part of Christianity. The first probable appearance of racism against Jews took place in Spain after the Reconquista of Toledo in 1449. That is roughly 1000 years after the end of Graeco-Roman heathenism and 500 years after the provisional termination of paganism at the other edges of Europe. Here we hear for the first time that Jews can be distinguished from Christians by the *limpieza de sangre* = "purity of blood" [Sic85].

The Nordic-Germanic myths tell nothing about anti-Judaism. As far as I know even the word "Jew" is not mentioned anywhere. By the way, it is difficult to see why Northern Europeans should be so hostile towards Jews for political or ideological reasons during the migration period or the early middle ages. A direct contact should have been rather minimal back then.

Ancient empires were hostile towards the Jewish religion to some extent. But that was not because Judaism was despised or supposed to be destroyed for religious, ideological or other reasons based on some faith. In fact, unlike pagans, monotheists usually refuse to participate in rituals from different religions like the state religion of such an ancient empire. Assmann describes this self-made segregation of one's own faith against other religions very well in his book "The Price of Monotheism" [Ass03]. In ancient times, first the Jews suffered under the lack of negative religious

---

[22] In this book the attribute "Nordic" is also just geographically meant, namely relative to Northern Europe, and not intended to describe an ethnicity.

freedom and later the Christians – but not because of a "wrong" faith they had but because of their refusal to participate in the social life of which the state religion was an integral part. This is of course no excuse or justification for discriminating behaviour, it only shows that back then a different motivation existed for those religious hostilities. Today we often assume other reasons due to later historical events.

Heathens had no other reason for the early anti-Judaism than this political and social one. That changed with the rising of Christianity and its accusation that the Jews were the "murderers of God", which gave anti-Judaism a new religious and ideological impetus. The reformer Martin Luther, often stylized as a folk hero, demanded in his writing „Of the Jews and their Jews" to burn their houses including the synagogues and schools, to destroy their property and possessions, to force them to work or to deport them and to forbid the rabbis to teach [Lut43].

The mythology contains neither a basis for racism nor for the leadership principle which is important for a national socialist or fascist social order. Although the Rigsmal contains a social system design which is impossible to achieve in today's democratic structures and, by the way, we should not even try to imposed, but a hierarchical structure with a single leader at the top is nowhere to be found. Although a political and legal body like the Thing was available, perhaps only for nobles and free men but not for servants, it was still for more democratic than the monarchist and absolutistic structures that came later. The strictly hierarchical structure of the absolutism is copied in the leadership principle of the Third Reich.

The previously mentioned mutuality which is inherent not only in the fundamental relationship between humans and Gods but also in the virtue of loyalty, directly contradicts such a strict hierarchy of command and unconditional obedience. Personally I cannot see how the Nordic-Germanic myths and the ethics and virtues extracted from them could nowadays propose or rationalise a leadership principle or racism.

Two exceptions are only those texts, which praise battles and war, and those which deal with virtues like courage, bravery and discipline. Such texts and the corresponding virtues can easily be exploited. An imagery of well-armed Gods fighting against the giant quickly provides an impressive propaganda material for warmongering and its justification. We must first forget though, that those martial images are symbolic and second, not at all the sole content of the myths. All this fighting is a symbol for the constant confrontation with nature and fate, of order against chaos and not a call to enrich oneself at others' expense or to extend one's political power on a large scale.

Since the mythological basis of ethics and morality as well as the political views derived from them needs a lot of interpretation, probably every religion could provide support for any political or ideological system. The impression that a pagan fundament exists in National-Socialism is mainly because plenty of pagan symbolism was used in Nazi Germany. Above all the runes, e.g. those used in the SS logo or those to symbolise the dates of birth and death (ᛉ and ᛦ instead of the usual symbols * and †).

By the way, contrary to popular opinion the swastika is neither a rune nor clearly of an "Aryan" origin. Its appearance is traceable in many cultures over the last 6000 years [Zen95], therefore it is not a typical Germanic symbol. "Swastika" is Sanskrit (स्वस्तिक) and means "bringer of good fortune". The Western world also regarded it as a symbol of luck before the NSDAP (*Nationalsozialistische deutsche Arbeiterpartei* = "German national socialist labour party") claimed it as its logo and later used it on the flag. The most interesting thesis on the swastika's origin is that a comet with four more or less symmetrically arranged core flares has shown up in the sky. Indeed, such a comet is depicted in a Chinese astronomical catalogue form the 3rd or 4th BC century [Sag85].

It is not surprising that within a certain culture a symbol is almost always interpreted with its most important meaning in that culture. While a swastika marks the location of Buddhist temples on Japanese maps (although its shape is mirrored), it is inevitably connected to National Socialism in the West. Why the latter is also done with other characters such as the runes is not that obvious. They did not have the central importance as the swastika in the

Third Reich and their origin and usage is definitely far older than any right-wing political conviction.

As the national socialist state sought a totalitarian assimilation of all aspects of life and its citizens, it has claimed, adapted and used all possible symbols, shapes, celebrations, holidays, social norms, arts and cultural elements. I think it is very questionable and precarious to suggest that people, who like art forms that were officially accepted in the Third Reich, would conform to such a political stance. Someone who likes a statue by Arno Breker or a movie starring Heinz Rühmann does not automatically need to be a follower of national socialist ideas. In fact, to assume such automatisms and to directly connect aesthetic feelings with political views looks exactly like a typical Nazi way of propaganda. It reminds one of the category "degenerate art" from that time period.

The thoughtless connection of certain artistic forms with the NS ideology occasionally brings forth strange fruits. In the right-wing scene labels in *Fraktur* are quite popular, and the public therefore quickly suspects the associated political stance if this kind of blackletter font is used on T-shirts, posters or patches. *Fraktur* or "Gothic script" was called "Jewish letters" in a 1941 circular letter by Martin Bormann, its use was forbidden for the official administration and schoolbooks were required to be switched to "normal font" as soon as possible [Bec06].

Now we want to answer the question as to how many heathens actually did exist during the Third Reich and how many of them were active within the government and upper administration. We do this to analyse the connection between paganism and National Socialism apart from the pure symbolism.

Yes, there were those who linked the rediscovery of pagan myths to nationalist ideas and the beginnings of the so-called *Neugermanentum* (= "neogermanism") in the 19th century. There were surely also those who followed a pagan religion and the National Socialist movement as well. I doubt though that they had any creative influence. Adolf Hitler explicitly warned against "so-called religious reformers with an old Germanic background" in a speech before the *Reichstag* in 1934 [Pus02] and called them "a group of folkish ideologists who believe the nation could only be made happy, if the experiences and results of two thousand years of history were neglected to start running around in bearskin again".

The census and other statistics from that period shed light on the distribution of religious beliefs within the German population. Unless otherwise stated all statistics mentioned in this chapter come from the publications of the Historical Commission to Berlin [Zip65].

Year	Protestant	Catholic	Jewish	Believing	Other
1925	64.12%	32.36%	0.90%	-	2.62%
1933	62.66%	32.46%	0.77%	-	4.11%
1939	48.72%	45.58%	-	3.09%	2.61%

Table 2: Third Reich religious denominations statistics

On the figures, it should be noted that the enormous increase in the ratio Catholics to Protestants between 1933 and 1939 was not due to a mass conversion but to the annexation of Austria, which had a predominantly Catholic population (and still has). In 1939, Jews were probably no longer counted or perhaps "jewish" was merged with "other". Roughly half of all German Jews emigrated at that time [Ben00] and the systematic mass homicide had not started yet. In 1939 the Jewish population might have been approximately 0.4%.

The classification "Believing" (*gottgläubig* = "believing in God") was introduced by and in the Third Reich for those who have left their church but still believed in God or at least pretended to do so [Die86]. It is synonymous with "undenominational" (*konfessionslos*), which is the normal official term, but avoids an atheist connotation. Atheism and materialism were seen in close connection with the allegedly Jewish communism; in his book "Mein Kampf" Hitler wrote of "atheist Jewish parties" [Hit38]. The NSDAP expected a commitment to God from its members, but no special denomination. Its policy programme, published in 1920, stated under topic 24 [His12a]: "The party as such considers a positive Christianity without a bond to a specific denomination. It fights the Jewish-materialistic spirit inside and outside of us." To describe yourself as a non-believer evoked suspicion of collusion with the Communists and Jews, thus non-high-ranking atheist Nazis would not have professed their atheism.

At the same time there was an effort to curtail the political influence of the churches in order to establish a totalitarian state. This became known as the so-called *Kirchenkampf* (= "church struggle") [Zip65]. A membership in an organisation which did not belong to the party or the state or was internationally active, such as the Roman Catholic Church, was not appreciated. People did not leave the church in vast numbers though. The above cited statistics show that the number of Catholics remained constant. The Protestant churches lost roughly 1.5% of the population between 1933 and 1938, which was at first counted as "Others" and from 1939 onwards categorised as "Believing". The total number of Christians remained roughly the same, it fell from 96.5% to 94.3%.

The denomination statistics of the *Reichstag* deputies show in more detail which religions the political leadership in the Third Reich followed and how this changed over time:

Year	Roman Catholic	Pro-testant	Old Catholic	No Stmt.	None	Other	Be-lieving
1933	144	501	1	13	1	-	-
1936	140	527	1	60	8	5	-
1938	157	374	2	132	3	7	180
1943	55	188	1	154	2	5	456

Table 3: *Reichstag* deputies religious denominations

In which of these categories may all the heathens who belonged to the Third Reich in droves have hidden? "Believing" was the designation of Christians and indifferent monotheists, who did not want to join a church, or atheists who were afraid to call themselves atheists. Reichstag deputies probably did not have as much to fear in this respect, so they could easily omit specifying their faith or mark it as "None", the latter was very rare though. Heathens may have called themselves "Believing" even though that contradicted the very meaning of that category at that time. (By the way, in German, *gottgläubig* would be some kind of grammatical error within paganism – correct would be *göttergläubig*.) However, I consider that very unlikely, especially if you look at the trend in the general population.

The last possible option is "Other", which held at the utmost 0.8% of all members of parliament in 1938. Details on those other religions and denominations were also collected. "Other" included: *Deutschkirche* ("German Church"), *deutschgläubig* (= "believing in German"), *Deutscher Gottesglaube* ("German Faith in God"), *Deutsche Gotterkenntnis* ("God knowledge") and "Creed: national-socialist". *Deutschkirche* most probably means the *Bund für Deutsche Kirche* (= "League for German Churches"), the predecessor of an anti-Semitic, protestant group called *Deutsche Christen* (= "German Christians") [Läc01]. *Deutschgläubig* might be an abbreviation for *Deutsche Glaubensbewegung* ("German Movement of Faith") created by Jakob Wilhelm Hauer [Ren92]. *Deutscher Gottesglaube* may point into the same direction; Hauer published a magazine called *Deutscher Glaube* (= "German Faith"). The *Bund für Deutsche Gotterkenntnis* was founded by Mathilde Ludendorff and proposed a pantheism without any involved cultic acts [Sch93]. It did not follow the old myths or Gods but thought that folklore should be regarded as an expression of divine aspects. That league was not taken seriously, the publishing of its writings were restricted by administrative measures, just like those of almost any other religious community [Zip65].

Of the folkish-pagan kind there could only have been the *Deutsche Glaubensbewegung* (DG) or perhaps to a very small extent the "League for German Churches". Hauer stated that the Germanic myths must be taken seriously, and talked of the faith in the "God within the world", which sounds a bit pantheistic after all. The NS management level distanced itself from Hauer by the way, thus he did not have any real influence [Ren92]. Several pagan associations joined in 1933 and formed the predecessor of the DG, the *Arbeitsgemeinschaft der Deutschen Glaubensbewegung* (= "study group of the DG"), including Ludwig Fahrenkrog's *Germanische Glaubensgemeinschaft* (= "Germanic Community of Faith"). However, it left the "study group" after its conversion into the DG in 1935 due to its increasing radicalisation [Wik12a]. In a report made by the SD (i.e. the security service of the SS) in 1934 the DG was mentioned as a part of the "Protestant movement" [Zip65].

Leaving the church was often carried out by members of the party and the SS; it was also propagated but never enforced. The ratios in the SS religious denominations statistics are very similar to those of the *Reichstag* deputies, though the documentation is incomplete for 1936:

Year	Protestant	Catholic	Believing	Other
1936	65.0%	23.0%	?	?
1937	60.0%	21.1%	18.7%	0.2%
1939	51.4%	22.6%	25.8%	0.2%

Table 4: SS religious denominations statistics

The SS members who had left the protestant church called themselves "believing" too. The number of "Others" is also negligibly small. In 1938 and 1939 half of the elitist National Socialists were protestant, a quarter Catholic and another quarter "believing".

In 1937 Hitler ordered his closest companions not to leave the church. Albert Speer said this was done for opportunistic reasons, and mentioned in this respect Göring and Goebbels by name [Spe93]. Hitler himself remained Catholic all his life.

The Protestants accepted National Socialism slightly more than the Catholics. That is not only proven by the number of SS-members, of whom the Protestants are a bit more and Catholic far less than the average, but also by the results of the votes during the Weimar Republic, in which the NSDAP scored higher in Protestants regions [Fal91].

Deutsche Christen was a Protestant group which propagated a synthesis of Christianity and National Socialism. One of its members was the theologian and *Reichsbischoff* ("[1st] Bishop of the Reich") of the German Protestant Church Ludwig Müller. Hitler considered the option of turning this Protestant church into a state church according to the English model, but thought bishop Müller was unsuitable to lead such a system. In table talks at the Obersalzberg he mentioned that the church was necessary for the state and that it would over time "adapt to the political goals of National Socialism", as "it by God always underwent such changes in history" [Spe93].

The desired synthesis of Christianity and National Socialism was already possible because of the Christian anti-Judaism, which had led to pogroms for a long time before the Third Reich. The Christian anti-Judaism mixed with 19th century racist ideologies provided the basis for the Holocaust and not a Nordic-Germanic paganism which had not formulated or handed down anything in this regard. We have already mentioned historical and ideological examples like Martin Luther's anti-Jewish writings.

It is surprising of course, how a Christian could be anti-Jewish, as the divine Jesus himself was a Jew. In fact there are some theories, or better yet conspiracy theories, which explain why this basic mythological fact should be wrong. For example Jesus' home is called Galilee because Gallic tribes had settled there[23]. He descended from these, therefore he was a Gaul and thus an Aryan [Goe09]. His childhood home Nazareth was an indication that he is a נזיר = "Nazir", which means something like "blessed" [Alf00]. In English it is called "Nazarite" or "Nazirite" (Num 6:19; in German *Nasiräer*). Now some even conclude, the word "Nazi" derive from that instead of being a disrespectful abbreviation.

Curate Walter Grundmann, member of *Deutsche Christen*, who retained his reputation as a theologian even in the GDR where he cooperated with the secret service [Bor09], declared that Jesus' race was irrelevant in their cause to "de-jewify" Christianity, as he was "God's miraculous recreation beyond all racial coincidences" [Gru34].

Hitler was probably not averse to the idea that Jesus was a Gaul [Goe09]. Though in "Mein Kampf" he only wrote that Jesus was not a Jew in essence but a declared enemy of Judaism, hence Christianity ought to fight Judaism too [Hit38]: "[The Jew's] spirit is inwardly alien to true Christianity, as his essence was alien to the

---

[23] Galilee derives in fact from the Hebrew word גליל = *galil* = "district", "borough" [Goo12].

great founder of the new doctrine. Of course he made no secret of his disposition towards the Jewish people, if necessary he swung the whip and drove the adversaries to humanity out of the Lord's temple. [...] For this, Jesus Christ was nailed to the cross, while our modern Christian parties degrade themselves [...] by doing political trafficking with atheist Jewish parties."

Christians today and then immediately see an appropriation of their faith and religion here. It has nothing to do with the real content of the religion and is in no way justifiable by historical or archaeological accounts. That pagan symbolism and content was appropriated in exactly the same way is not recognised though. It is easier to recognise such appropriated in your own environment than in areas which are alien or not accepted.

Heinrich Himmler and the SS led by him are of special interest. Both are considered outstanding examples for the socially relevant role of neopaganism or neogermanism in the Third Reich, and they do show some pagan aspects.

Himmler also came from a Catholic family and had openly expressed his reluctance of Christianity. He promoted the church struggle within the ranks of the SS, which can be seen in the 25% who left the church. Whether he himself had left the church or followed the above mentioned Führer's order to stay in it, I could not determine.

Undeniably Himmler was interested in paganism and its history. Certainly, he shared some views on historical events and notables with present and former pagans.

For example, Himmler called Charlemagne several times "Butcher of the Saxons", a notion that refers to the Bloody Verdict of Verden in which 4500 Saxons were executed during the Saxon Wars [Kur95], even though science doubts the magnitude and location [Bip89]. Undeniable however is the death penalty for being a heathen or to refuse to become baptised as laid down in the terms of surrender after the Saxon Wars; see point 8 of the *capitulatio de partibus saxoniae* [Mun04]. Because of this legislation Charlemagne is not very popular in pagan circles as well. The following quote uttered by Hitler however shows in a very insightful way how other leaders thought about the first German Emperor [Spe93]: "This Himmler has again held a speech in which he called Charlemagne 'Butcher of the Saxons'. The death of those many Saxons was not a historic crime, as Himmler deems; Charlemagne did very well to subdue Widukind and to kill the Saxons without further ado, for by all this he has enabled the Frankish Empire and thus the Western culture to enter current Germany." Along with Hitler, the Waffen-SS also did not dislike Charles that much as Himmler. A French volunteer division was named after the emperor, the 33rd Grenadier-Division of the SS (1st French) *Charlemagne* [Qua90].

Furthermore the symbolism utilised by the SS and specially introduced rituals for weddings, Christmas etc. have similarities with their pagan roots which of course heathens were and are still using and performing. Many things were especially designed for the SS based on historical templates and have completely replaced the originals designs in the public perception. This makes a distinction between general pagan and particular national-socialist items extremely difficult.

The SS-logo for example is not a traditional symbol but was created on the basis of the rune Sowilo by the graphic designer Walter Heck [Yen10]. Neither the stroke nor the alleged meanings of the runes were of ancient origin but came from the works of the mystic Guido von List [Lis12]. While in the early middle ages the Sowilo-Rune was a sign for the sun, von List called it "Sigrune" and assigned it to victory (= *Sieg* in German) and several other things.

Candlesticks bearing matching symbols for the SS-internal Christmas celebrations and individual home altars were produced, the so-called *Julleuchter* (= "Yule lantern"). It is doubtful whether those devices and the associated tradition really came from a pagan source [Nor12]. The earliest archaeological findings date from the 16th century and have been found in Halland, Sweden. So they were built roughly 500 years after the complete Christianization of Sweden and were named after the Swedish word for Christmas (*jul*) not for solstice (*solstånd* [Goo12]). The latter name might be more suitable and likely for a heathen origin.

Another example is the sign of the "Black Sun" representing a sun wheel with jagged rays, which decorates the *Obergruppenführers*' hall in the Wewelsburg at Paderborn as a floor ornament. The castle Wewelsburg was a central SS facility during the Third Reich, and *Obergruppenführer* is an SS rank equating to a general in the army. This icon appears in both the political right-wing and the neo-folk music scene. Like paganism itself the latter group is not generally a group of right-wing extremists as many assume because of the utilised symbolism. The model for the Black Sun symbol are Alemannic trinkets from the late migration period [Web08]. There is a very similar Bajuvarian disc with twelve rays and a swastika counter-clockwise at the center [Haa12]. The well-known and commonly used form of the Black Sun today also has twelve rays looking like three overlapping swastikas. This evidently differs from the Alemannic historical ones, the rays increased from five to nine. It was designed by the mystic and leading SS-member Karl Maria Wiligut, who has also designed the SS *Totenkopfring* (= "Skull Ring") [Lon08]. Indeed, Wiligut could be called a heathen, though most of his views might cause the pagan community to shake their heads, e.g. he claimed to be a direct descendent of the Æsir. To learn more on Wiligut's intellectual abilities I recommend reading his letter of application to the SS, which is displayed at the Wewelsburg SS museum ("Erinnerungs- und Gedenkstätte Wewelsburg 1933-1945" [Wew12]). It would probably even hinder one from getting a position as an apprentice today due to the many typographical errors.

All this symbolism shows that the SS and especially Himmler had an enormous interest in history, in particular the history of the German people. The SS had a department called *Ahnenerbe* (= "Inheritance of the Forefathers"), which conducted archaeological expeditions and historical studies. A well-known representative of this subsidiary organisation was Otto Rahn, who in the 1930s examined the Cathars in France and the crusade fought against them in the 13th century. His literary work on that matter [Rah06] is still accepted today. Afterwards, Rahn had to do his duty in the concentration camp Buchenwald at the time of the *Reichskristallnacht*, the vast pogrom in 1938 also called the "Night of

Broken Glass". He then left the SS and most likely committed suicide half a year later, although that has not been completely confirmed [Kat99].

So, there were indeed some neopagan tendencies in the National Socialist Movement, in particular in the SS. But these were essentially derived from esoteric circles emerging in the 19th century and in parallel to the rediscovery and reintegration of Nordic-Germanic mythology into the cultural inventory. A link to ancient history is missing. A similar gap exists in the theological and racist efforts of the group *Deutsche Christen* to combine National Socialism and Christianity.

A truly religious connection cannot be recognized, neither in the original and ancient nor in the modern sense explained in this book. Many symbols and some newly designed celebrations were based on archaeological findings, but they were virtually all professionally created. Nowadays, modern Heathenism is also forced to re-invent a lot, because the historical base is missing and the archaeological findings do not really help to recreate a rite. The objective behind all this, however, is a completely different one.

The reason for the promotion of pagan signs and rites was far more likely the support of the Third Reich's struggle with the church in order to move people in large numbers from non-governmental organisations to those of the state and the party than to actually introduce a truly pagan religion. This is confirmed by the nationalist Christian groups, the secularism camouflaged as "believing" and the extremely low popularity of other religions besides Christianity among the population, the party and the SS.

Himmler and some high ranking SS members were very interested in Nordic-Germanic paganism, but they were also interested in Buddhism and Islam. The SS, for example, supported various scientific and mountaineering expeditions to Tibet [Mie06]. One of those Tibet expeditions got worldwide recognition from the book of its participant Heinrich Harrer and its adaption to film [Har06].

There are some quotes on this complex subject by Adolf Hitler, the Supreme Commander of everyone and everything back then, which clearly show how he thought about it and what kind of ideas he had on the religious orientation of the Reich and its people.

On the esoteric and neopagan aspects, regarding Himmler's ideas here [Spe93]: "What nonsense! Now we have finally come so far to leave all mysticism behind, and he is starting anew. For that we could stick to the Church that has at least a tradition."

Although Hitler never left the Catholic Church, he obviously did not share her faith. The following paragraph from "Mein Kampf" illustrates that the Catholic faith was not his, and it also shows his admiration for the fact that the Church taught scientifically disproven dogmas as irrefutable truth for two millennia and will most probably do so in the future. He regarded this as a role model for the nationalist movement and its followers [Hit38]: "Here we can learn from the Catholic Church as well. Although her system of theories contradicts exact science and research in some points, she is still not willing to sacrifice even a little syllable of their dogmas. She correctly acknowledges that her toughness [result from] the strict adherence to once written-down dogmas, which brings the character of faith to everything. Thus she stands firmer as ever."

He continues that a serious and victorious nationalist movement needed such firmly formulated principles without "making concessions to the zeitgeist". The difference between primary religions without such written-down principles like Heathenism and other concepts of faith should be obvious.

References to Islam can be found in the Third Reich too. The SS had a completely Muslim division, the 13th Mountain-Division, also called "Handschar" after an Arabian scimitar [Qua90]. An epithet was "1st Croatian" but it consisted of Bosnian volunteers, wearing the SS-skull on their fez. Its mobilisation was supported by Muhammad Amin al-Husayni, the Grand Mufti of Jerusalem, who lived in Berlin from 1941 onwards and was a member of the SS [Dah08]. (Hence I wonder, whether he described himself as "Believing" or "Others" in the SS denomination statistics.) After the lost battle of El-Alamein in 1942, he called for Jihad against the Jews.

Hitler himself had quite a positive attitude towards Islam. According to Albert Speer, he liked the idea that the world would have become Islamic if the Arabs invading Europe in the 8th century had beaten Karl Martell in the battle of Poitiers [Spe93]: “They would have imposed a religion onto the Germanic peoples, which would have suited them very well, because it teaches to spread faith by the sword and to subjugate all nations under its rule. Due to their racial inferiority the conquerors would not have prevailed against the German, who were used to the rough nature of their homelands, so that in the end […] the Muslim German would have led a worldwide Islamic empire.” In comparison Christianity was not that suitable in his opinion, paganism is not mentioned at all. “We do have the misfortune to belong to a wrong religion. […] The Muslim religion would be much more appropriate for us than Christianity with this sloppy tolerance.”

A final quote from Alfred Rosenberg in his famous and besides Hitler’s “Mein Kampf” the most influential book of the national-socialist movement “Der Mythus des 20. Jahrhunderts” [Pip05], [Ros30]: “They concealed, that I declared Wotanism as a dead religion […], and insinuated falsely and dishonestly, that I wanted to recreate the ‘pagan Wotan’s cult’.”

BIBLIOGRAPHY

[Alf00] Alan F. Alford; When The Gods Came Down – The Catastrophic Roots of Religion Revealed; Hodder & Stoughton; 2000

[Ass03] Jan Assmann; Die Mosaische Unterscheidung – Oder der Preis des Monotheismus; Carl Hanser; 2003

[Ass07] Jan Assmann; Monotheismus und die Sprache der Gewalt; 4th edition; Picus; 2007

[Bec06] Friedrich Beck: „Schwabacher Judenlettern" – Schriftverruf im Third Reich; in: Botho Brachmann (Hrsg.); Die Kunst des Vernetzens; Verlag für Berlin-Brandenburg; 2006

[Bed43] Beda venerabilis; The Complete Works of Venerable Bede, Vol. VI; Whittaker and Co.; 1843

[Ben00] Wolfgang Benz; Geschichte des Third Reiches. C.H. Beck; 2000

[Ben06] Herbert Benson et al.; Study of the Therapeutic Effects of Intercessory Prayer (STEP) in Cardiac Bypass Patients; American Heart Journal 151, Nr. 4; 2006

[Bib12] Bibelserver Webseite (http://www.bibleserver.com); Date: May 2012

[Bip89] Wilhelm von Bippen; Die Hinrichtung der Sachsen durch Karl den Grossen; in: Deutsche Zeitschrift für Geschichtswissenschaft 1; 1889

[Bla05] Olaf Blanke et al.; Linking Out-of-Body Experience and Self Processing to Mental Own-Body Imagery at the Temporoparietal Junction; The Journal of Neuroscience 25, Nr. 3; 2005

[Blo78] Ned Block; Troubles with Functionalism; in: Perception and Cognition; University of Minnesota Press; 1978

[Boe47] Boethius; De persona et duabus naturis; in: Jacques Paul Migne (Hrsg.); Patrologia Latina 70, 1342–5; Paris; 1847

[Boo03] Helmut de Boor; Das Nibelungenlied – Zweisprachig; 5th edition; Parkland; 2003

[Bor09] Lukas Bormann; Walter Grundmann und das Ministerium für Staatssicherheit. Chronik einer Zusammenarbeit aus Überzeugung (1956 bis 1969); in: Kirchliche Zeitgeschichte 22; 2009

[Bre06] Eric D. Brenner, Rainer Stahlberg, Stefano Mancuso, Jorge Vivanco, František Baluška, Elizabeth Van Volkenburg; Plant neurobiology: an integrated view of plant signaling; Trends in Plant Science 11 (8); 2006

[Bud04] Stephanie L. Budin; A Reconsideration of the Aphrodite-Ashtart Syncretism; Numen 51, 2; 2004
[Bul98] Rudolf Bultmann; Das Urchristentum; Patmos Paperback 1998
[Car95] Carmina Burana; 6th edition; dtv; 1995
[Car06] E.R. Carmin; Das schwarze Reich; Nikol; 2006
[Car09] Bernard Carr; Universe or Multiverse?; Cambridge University Press; 2009
[Car12] Titus Lucretius Carus; De Rerum Natura Liber II; WikiSource (http://la.wikisource.org/wiki/De_rerum_natura_%28Titus_Lucretius_Carus%29/Liber_II); Date: April 2012
[Cic95] Marcus Tullius Cicero; De natura deorum – Über das Wesen der Götter; Reclam; 1995
[Cot08] Arthur Cotterell; Mythologie – Götter, Helden, Mythen; Parragon Books; 2008
[Dah08] David G. Dalin, John F. Rothmann; Icon of Evil – Hitler's Mufti and the Rise of Radical Islam; Random House; 2008
[Dan06] David W. Daniels; Babylon Religion; Chick Publications; 2006
[Daw07] Richard Dawkins; Der Gotteswahn; Ullstein; 2007
[Die07] Hermann Diels; Die Fragmente der Vorsokratiker; Weidmann; 1907
[Die86] Margarete Dierks; Jakob Wilhelm Hauer; Heidelberg; 1986
[Doc01] Jan Dochhorn; Zur Entstehungsgeschichte der Religion bei Euhemeros – Mit einem Ausblick auf Philo von Byblos; in: Zeitschrift für Religions- und Geistesgeschichte 4; 2001
[Eis04] Rudolf Eisler; Wörterbuch der philosophischen Begriffe; Berlin; 1904
[Fal91] Jürgen W. Falter; Hitlers Wähler; C.H. Beck; 1991
[Feu41] Ludwig Feuerbach; Das Wesen des Christentums; Leipzig; 1841
[Fin04] Israel Finkelstein und Neil A. Silberman; Keine Posaunen vor Jericho: Die archäologische Wahrheit über die Bibel; dtv; 2004
[Fir12] Lucius Caecilius Firmianus; Divinarum Institutionum Liber IV – De Vera Sapientia et Religione; Documenta Catholica Omnia (http://www.documentacatholicaomnia.eu); Date: May 2012
[Fla00] Quintus Horatius Flaccus; Sermones, Epistulae; Artemis & Winkler; 2007
[For12] Forn Siðr Webseite (http://www.fornsidr.dk); Date: April 2012

[Frü99] Sigrid Früh; Rauhnächte – Märchen, Brauchtum, Aberglaube; 5th edition; Stendel; 1999
[Fry05] Richard Frye; Ibn Fadlan's Journey to Russia; Markus Wiener Publishing; 2005
[Gau93] Gautama Buddha; Die Lehrreden des Buddha aus der Angereihten Sammlung: Anguttara-Nikaya, Band 3; 5th edition; J. Kamphausen; 1993
[Gem86] Albert Gemoll; Die Homerischen Hymnen; B.G. Teubner; 1886
[Gol05a] David Theo Goldberg; Ethnocentrism; in: Maryanne Cline Horowitz (Hrsg.); New Dictionary of the History of Ideas; Thomson Galc; 2005
[Goe09] Hajo Goertz; Der Mythos vom arischen Jesus (http://www.dradio.de/dkultur/sendungen/religionen/993359/); 2009
[Gol05b] David M. Goldenberg; The Curse of Ham – Race and Slavery in Early Judaism, Christianity, and Islam; Princeton University Press; 2005
[Goo00] Nicholas Goodrick-Clarke; Die okkulten Wurzeln des Nationalsozialismus; 2nd edition; Stocker; 2000
[Goo07] Felicitas D. Goodman; Wo die Geister auf den Winden reiten; Neuauflage; Binkey Kok; 2007
[Goo12] Google Übersetzer (http://translate.google.de); Date: May 2012
[Gri35] Jacob Grimm; Deutsche Mythologie; Dieterichsche Buchhandlung; 1835
[Gri12] Jacob und Wilhelm Grimm; Deutsches Wörterbuch; Akademie der Wissenschaften zu Göttingen (http://woerterbuchnetz.de/DWB/); Date: April 2012
[Gru34] Walter Grundmann; Totale Kirche im totalen Staat; Dresden; 1934
[Gut99] Alan Guth; Dic Geburt des Kosmos aus dem Nichts – Die Theorie des inflationären Universums; Knaur; 1999
[Haa12] Museum des Haager Landes, 1. Geschoß (http://www.museum-haag.de/index.php/das-museum/rundgang-durchs-museum/51-erstes-stockwerk); Date: July 2012
[Hag12] haGalil.com (http://www.hagalil.com/judentum/torah/zwi-braun/5-vaet-02.htm); Date: April 2012

[Har80] Michael Harner; The Way of the Shaman: A Guide to Power and Healing; Harper & Row; 1980
[Har06] Heinrich Harrer; Sieben Jahre in Tibet – Mein Leben am Hofe des Dalai Lama; Ullstein; 2006
[Haw88] Stephen W. Hawking; Eine kurze Geschichte der Zeit – Die Suche nach der Urkraft des Universums; Bertelsmann; 1988
[Hei27] Werner Heisenberg; Über den anschaulichen Inhalt der quantentheoretischen Kinematik und Mechanik; in Zeitschrift für Physik, 43, Nr. 3; 1927
[Hei55] Werner Heisenberg; The Development of the Interpretation of the Quantum Theory; in Wolgang Pauli (Hrsg.); Niels Bohr and the Development of Physics, 35; Pergamon Press; 1955
[Her85] Ursula Hermann, Horst Leisering und Heinz Hellerer; Knaurs großes Wörterbuch der deutschen Sprache – Der große Störig; Droemer Knaur; 1985
[Her13] Hero of Camelot; Bede's 'Ecclesiastical History of the English People' (http://www.heroofcamelot.com/docs/Bede-Ecclesiastical-History.pdf); Date: June 2013
[Hes99] Hesiod; Theogonie; Reclam; 1999
[Hin89] Christoph Hinckeldey; Justiz in alter Zeit; Rothenburg; 1989
[His12a] Historisches Lexikon Bayerns (http://www.historisches-lexikon-bayerns.de/document/artikel_44553_bilder_value_1_nsdap.jpg); Date: July 2012
[His12b] Historisches Lexikon Bayerns – Thule-Gesellschaft, 1918-1933 (http://www.historisches-lexikon-bayerns.de/artikel/artikel_44318); Date: July 2012
[Hit38] Adolf Hitler; Mein Kampf; 330th – 334th edition; Franz Eher Nachf.; 1938
[Höf61] Otto Höfler; Siegfried, Arminius und die Symbolik; Winter; 1961
[Höf08] Otfried Höffe; Lexikon der Ethik; 7th edition; C.H. Beck; 2008
[Hof07] Peter Hoffmann; Claus Schenk Graf von Stauffenberg – Die Biographie; Pantheon; 2007
[Hom09] Homer; Ilias; Anaconda; 2009
[Hux89] Thomas Henry Huxley; Agnosticism; Popular Science Monthly, Volume 34; April 1889
[Imd12] IMDb (http://www.imdb.de/title/tt0120657/); Date: May 2012

[Jon95] David E. H. Jones; Zittergas und schräges Wasser – Die phantastischen Erfindungen des modernen Daedalus; 7th edition; Harry Deutsch; 1995
[Jor01] Wilhelm Jordan; Edda – Die heiligen Lieder der Ahnen; 3rd edition; Arun; 2001
[Jos11] Flavius Josephus; Jüdische Altertümer; 3rd edition; Marix; 2011
[Jun01] Carl Gustav Jung; Archetypen; dtv; 2001
[Kan81] Immanuel Kant; Critik der reinen Vernunft; Johann Friedrich Hartknoch; 1781
[Kan84] Immanuel Kant; Beantwortung der Frage: Was ist Aufklärung?; Berlinische Monatsschrift 4; 1784
[Kat99] Winfried Katholing; Heilige Stätten der Heiden und Ketzer – Ein Führer zu ausgewählten Kultplätzen in Deutschland und Frankreich; Aschaffenburg; 1999
[Kel98] James G. Kellas; The politics of nationalism and ethnicity; 2nd edition; MacMillan; 1998
[Kha07] Tipu V. Khan, Safa Shakir-Shatnawi Khan, Andre Akhondi, Teepu W. Khan; White Coat Hypertension: Relevance to Clinical and Emergency Medical Services Personnel; Medscape General Medicine 9(1); 2007
[Kim05] Jaegwon Kim; Philosophy of Mind; 2nd edition; Westview Press; 2005
[Kla95] Hans-Josef Klauck; Die religiöse Umwelt des Urchristentums I – Stadt- und Hausreligion, Mysterienkulte, Volksglaube; Kohlhammer; 1995
[Kla96] Hans-Josef Klauck; Die religiöse Umwelt des Urchristentums II – Herrscher- und Kaiserkult, Philosophie, Gnosis; Kohlhammer; 1996
[Kle10] Zalika Klemenc-Ketis, Janko Kersnik und Stefek Grmec ; The effect of carbon dioxide on near-death experiences in out-of-hospital cardiac arrest survivors: a prospective observational study; Critical Care 14 2; 2010
[Klo06] Hans Kloft; Mysterienkulte der Antike – Götter, Menschen, Rituale; 3rd edition; C.H. Beck; 2006
[Kru06] Mitchell W. Krucoff, Suzanne W. Crater, Kerry L. Lee; From efficacy to safety concerns: A STEP forward or a step back for clinical research and intercessory prayer?; American Heart Journal 151, Nr. 4; 2006

[Kur95] Friedrich Kurze (Hrsg.); Scriptores rerum Germanicarum in usum scholarum separatim editi 6: Annales regni Francorum inde ab a. 741 usque ad a. 829, qui dicuntur Annales Laurissenses maiores et Einhardi; Monumenta Germaniae Historica; 1895
[Läc01] Rainer Lächele: Germanisierung des Christentums – Heroisierung Christi; in: Stefanie von Schnurbein, Justus H. Ulbricht (Hrsg.); Völkische Religion und Krisen der Moderne. Entwürfe „arteigener" Glaubenssysteme seit der Jahrhundertwende; Königshausen und Neumann; 2001
[Lei10] Gottfried Wilhelm Leibniz; Essais de théodicée; 1710
[Lem27] Georges Lemaître; Un univers homogen de mass constante et de rayon croissant, rendant compte de la vitesse radial des nebuleuses extra-galactiques; in Annales de la Société scientifique de Bruxelles, Tome XLVII, série A; 1927
[Lew29] Clarence Irving Lewis; Mind and the World Order – Outline of a Theory of Knowledge; Charles Scribner's Sons; 1929
[Lew82] Bernard Lewis; Race and Slavery in the Middle East – An Historical Enquiry; Oxford University Press; 1982
[Lis12] Guido von List; Das Geheimnis der Runen – Was die Runen wirklich bedeuten!; 2nd edition; DHV; 1912
[Lok01] Ernst Lokowandt; Shinto: Eine Einführung; Iudicium; 2001
[Lon08] Peter Longerich; Heinrich Himmler – Biographie; Siedler; 2008
[Lut43] Martin Luther; Von den Juden und ihren Lügen (http://archive.org/details/VonDenJudenUndIhrenLuegen); Wittenberg; 1543
[Mar99] Miroslav Marcovich (Hrsg.); Diogenis Laertii Vitae Philosophorum, Band 1; B.G. Teubner; 1999
[Mar10] Christoph Markschies; Die Gnosis; 3rd edition; C.H. Beck; 2010
[Mar12] Marvel Webseite (http://marvel.com/movies/movie/36/thor); Date: May 2012
[Mie06] Peter Mierau; Nationalsozialistische Expeditionspolitik – Deutsche Asien-Expeditionen 1933–1945; Herbert Utz; 2006
[Mue77] Gerhard Müller; Theologische Realenzyklopädie; Walther de Gruyter & Co.; 1977
[Mue87] Karl Müller, Theo Sundermeier; Lexikon missionstheologischer Grundbegriffe; Reimer; 1987

[Mun47] Peter Andreas Munch,Carl Rikard Unger; Saemundar-Edda; P.T. Mallings; 1847
[Mun04] Dana Carleton Munro; Selections from the Laws of Charles the Great; Neuauflage; Kessinger Publishing; 2004
[Nea43] August Neander; Allgemeine Geschichte der christlichen Religion und Kirche, Band 3; Friedrich Perthes; 1843
[Noe99] Daniel C. Noel; Soul of Shamanism: Western Fantasies, Imagined Realities; Continuum International; 1999
[Nor12] Nornirs Ætt; Der Julleuchter – eine erfundene „Tradition" (http://www.nornirsaett.de/der-julleuchter-eine-erfundene-tradition/); Date: July 21012
[Obe98] Thomas Oberlies; Die Religion des Rig-Veda; Wien; 1998
[Pas99] Blaise Pascal; Über die Religion und über einige andere Gegenstände (Pensées); 9th edition; Schneider Lambert; 1999
[Pau18] Pausanias; Description of Greece with an English Translation; Harvard University Press; 1918
[Pip05] Ernst Piper; Alfred Rosenberg – Hitlers Chefideologe; Karl Blessing; 2005
[Poe12] The Poetic Edda (http://www.sacred-texts.com/neu/poe/); Date: December 2012
[Pop78] Karl Popper; Three Worlds – The Tanner Lecture on Human Values; University of Michigan; 1978
[Pus02] Uwe Puschner; Ein Volk, ein Reich, ein Gott. Völkische Weltanschauung und Bewegung; 2008; in: Bernd Sösemann (Hrsg.); Der Nationalsozialismus und die deutsche Gesellschaft; München; 2002
[Qua90] Bruce Quarrie; Das große Buch der Deutschen Heere im 20. Jahrhundert; Podzun-Pallas; 1990
[Rab89] Horst Rabe; Reich und Glaubensspaltung, Deutschland 1500 – 1600; Büchergilde Gutenberg; 1989
[Rag03] Lord Raglan; The Hero – A Study in Tradition, Myth and Drama; Dover Publications; 2003
[Rah06] Otto Rahn; Kreuzzug gegen den Gral – Die Geschichte der Albigenser; Zeitenwende; 2006
[Rau94] Reinhold Rau; Briefe des Bonifatius, Willibalds Leben des Bonifatius – Bonifatii epistulae, Willibaldi vita Bonifatii; Wissenschaftliche Buchgesellschaft; 1994
[Ree11] Martin Rees; Universum; Dorling Kindersley München; 2011

[Reh05] Shakaib U. Rehman, Paul J. Nietert, Dennis W. Cope, Anne Osborne Kilpatrick; What to wear today? Effect of doctor's attire on the trust and confidence of patients; The American Journal of Medicine, 118; 2005
[Ren92] Karl Rennstich; Der Deutsche Glaube – Jakob Wilhelm Hauer (1881-1962): Ein Ideologe des Nationalsozialismus; Evangelische Zentralstelle für Weltanschauungsfragen, Information Nr. 121 Stuttgart XII; 1992
[Rie93] Julien Ries; Ursprung der Religionen; Pattloch; 1993
[Rom12] The Roman Baths (http://www.romanbaths.co.uk); Date: July 2012
[Ros90] Wilhelm Heinrich Roscher; Ausführliches Lexikon der griechischen und römischen Mythologie; Band 1, Abt. 2; B.G. Teubner; 1890
[Ros30] Alfred Rosenberg; Der Mythus des 20. Jahrhunderts; Hoheneichen; 1930
[Rus03] Bertrand Russel; The Principles of Mathematics; Cambridge University Press; 1903
[Rus18] Bertrand Russell: The Philosophy of Logical Atomism; in The Collected Papers of Bertrand Russell, Band 8; 1918
[Saa95] Holger Saal; Das Symbol als Leitmodell für religiöses Verstehen: tiefenpsychologische Theoriemodelle und ihre Konsequenzen in didaktischen Vermittlungsprozessen; Vandenhoeck und Ruprecht; 1995
[Sag82] Carl Sagan; Unser Kosmos; Droemer Knaur; 1982
[Sag85] Carl Sagan, Ann Druyan; Der Komet; Droemer Knaur; 1985
[Sch05] Emil Schürer; Die siebentägige Woche im Gebrauch der christlichen Kirche der ersten Jahrhunderte; in: Probeheft der Zeitschrift für die neutestamentliche Wissenschaft, Jahrgang 6; 1905
[Sch23] Leopold von Schroeder; Arische Religion, Band 1; Leipzig; 1923
[Sch65] Einar von Schuler; Die Mythologie der Hethiter und Hurriter; in: Hans Wilhelm Haussig (Hrsg.); Wörterbuch der Mythologie, Band 1: Götter und Mythen im Vorderen Orient; Klett-Cotta; 1965
[Sch82] Gustav Schwab; Sagen des klassischen Altertums; Droemer Knaur; 1982
[Sch93] Stefanie von Schnurbein; Göttertrost in Wendezeiten; München; 1993

[Sch95] Werner H. Schmidt; Einführung in das Alte Testament; 5th edition; Walther de Gruyter & Co.; 1995
[Sch02] Eckhard J. Schnabel; Urchristliche Mission; TVG; 2002
[Sha91] Byron E. Shafer, John R. Baines, Leonard H. Lesko, David Silverman; Religion in Ancient Egypt: Gods, Myths, and Personal Practice; Cornell University Press; 1991
[Sic85] Albert A. Sicroff; Los Estatutos de Limpieza de Sangre; Taurus Ediciones S. A.; 1985
[Sig10] Sigríður Sunna Ebenesersdóttir et al.; A New Subclade of mtDNA Haplogroup C1 Found in Icelanders: Evidence of Pre-Columbian Contact?; American Journal of Physical Anthropology, Wiley-Blackwell; November 2010
[Sim76] Karl Joseph Simrock; Die Edda; J.G. Cotta; 1876
[Sim06a] Rudolf Simek; Götter und Kulte der Germanen; 2nd edition; C.H. Beck; 2006
[Sim06b] Rudolf Simek; Lexikon der germanischen Mythologie; 3rd edition; Kröner; 2006
[Spa81] James B. Spamer: The kenning and the kend heiti – A contraste study of periphrasis in two Germanic poetic traditions; Ann Arbor; 1981
[Spe93] Albert Speer; Erinnerungen; Ullstein; 1993
[Spi03] Friedrich Spiro; Pausaniae Graeciae Descriptio; B.G. Teubner; 1903
[Stä06] Otto Stählin; Clemens Alexandrinus II – Stromata I-VI; J.C. Hinrichs; 1906
[Ste01] Ephraim Stern; Archaeology of the Land of the Bible, Vol. 2; New York; 2001
[Ste04] Fritz Steinbock; Das heilige Fest – Rituale des traditionellen germanischen Heidentums in heutiger Zeit; Daniel Junker; 2004
[Sno91] Snorri Sturluson; Prosa-Edda – Altisländische Göttergeschichten; Manesse; 1991
[Sym73] Quintus Aurelius Symmachus; Prefect and emperor – The Relationes of Symmachus; Clarendon Press; 1973
[Tac92] Publius Cornelius Tacitus; Annalen XI-XVI; Reclam; 1992
[Tac07] Publius Cornelius Tacitus; Germania; Reclam; 2007
[Thi77] Paul Thieme; Gedichte aus dem Rig-Veda; Reclam; 1977
[Tho58] Stith Thompson; Motif-index of folk-literature: a classification of narrative elements in folktales, ballads, myths, fables, mediaeval

romances, exempla, fabliaux, jest-books, and local legends; Indiana University Press; 1958
[Uex08] Thure von Uexküll, Wolf Langewitz; Das Placebo-Phänomen; in: Psychosomatische Medizin: Modelle ärztlichen Denkens und Handelns; Elsevier; 2008
[Uss50] James Ussher; Annales veteris testamenti, a prima mundi origine deducti; 1650
[Vat65] 2. Vatikanisches Konzil; Nostra Aetate – Über das Verhältnis der Kirche zu den nichtchristlichen Religionen; 1965
[Vil07] Alex Vilenkin; Many Worlds in One – The Search for Other Universes; Macmillan Us; 2007
[Vor07] Jacobus de Voragine; Die Legenda aurea; 14th edition; Gütersloher Verlagshaus; 2007
[Vri61] Jan de Vries; Forschungsgeschichte der Mythologie; Orbis academicus I, 7; Karl Alber; 1961
[Wal03] Robert J. Wallis; Shamans/Neo-Shamans: Ecstasies, Alternative Archaeologies and Contemporary Pagans; Taylor & Francis; 2003
[Web08] Web-Archiv; SS-Architektur (http://web.archive.org/web/20080627160900/http://www.ns-gedenkstaetten.de/nrw/de/wewelsburg/thema_3/ss_architektur.html); archived: 2008-06-27
[Wei77] Steven Weinberg; Die ersten drei Minuten – Der Ursprung des Universums; dtv; 1977
[Wer74] Jürgen Werner, Herbert Greiner-Mai; Lukian – Werke in drei Bänden; Aufbau; 1974
[Wew12] Erinnerungs- und Gedenkstätte Wewelsburg 1933-1945 (http://www.wewelsburg.de/de/wewelsburg-1933-1945/einstieg.php); Date: July 2012
[Wik12a] WikiPedia: Deutsche_Glaubensbewegung (http://de.wikipedia.org/wiki/Deutsche_Glaubensbewegung); Date: July 2012
[Wik12b] WikiPedia: Isis (http://de.wikipedia.org/wiki/Isis_%28%C3%84gyptische_Mythologie%29); Date: June 2012
[Wik12c] WikiPedia: Nīþ (http://en.wikipedia.org/wiki/N%C4%AB%C3%BE); Date: September 2012

[Wik12d] WikiPedia: Wicca (Ethik)
(http://de.wikipedia.org/wiki/Wicca#Ethik); Date: September 2012
[Wil77] Dietrich Wildung; Imhotep und Amenhotep – Gottwerdung im alten Ägypten; Deutscher Kunstverlag; 1977
[Wol10] Fritz Wolff; Avesta – Die heiligen Bücher der Parsen; Strassburg; 1910
[Xen88] Xenophanes; Die Fragmente; Artemis & Winkler; 1988
[Yen10] Bill Yenne; Hitler's Master of the Dark Arts – Himmler's Black Knights and the Occult Origins of the SS; Zenith Press; 2010
[Zen95] Christian Zentner; Friedemann Bedürftig; Das große Lexikon des Dritten Reiches; Weltbild; 1995
[Zip65] Friedrich Zipfel; Kirchenkampf in Deutschland 1933 – 1945; Veröffentlichungen der Historischen Kommission zu Berlin, Band 11; Walther de Gruyter & Co.; 1965

List of Tables and Figures

Table 1: Identification of Roman with German Gods by the names of the weekdays 61
Table 2: Third Reich religious denominations statistics 146
Table 3: *Reichstag* deputies religious denominations 147
Table 4: SS religious denominations statistics 149

Figure 1: Frequent god-conceptions in primary and secondary religions 22
Figure 2: God-conceptions of other religious types 24
Figure 3: Setting of a secondary religion 28
Figure 4: Setting of a primary religion 29
Figure 5: Basic pagan god-conceptions 54

If the figures are not sufficiently recognisable for the reader in the printed form: On http://andreas-mang.de/en/nr2/abb.html they can be downloaded in high resolution for private use and improved visibility.

INDEX

Achilles 36, 130
Aeneas 117
Æsir 118
Ahriman 132
Ahura Mazda 132
Altar of the Unknown God 59
Altar of Victory 137
Andhrímnir 95
Apollo 130
Apollon 58, 120
apotheosis 50
archetype
  mythological 33
Aristarchus 20
Arminius 35
Asatru 133
Ásatrúarfélagið 134
Ashtoreth 51
Ask 44
Assmann, Jan 18, 22, 31
Astarte 51
Attis 59
Atum 42
Audhumbla 39
Avesta Yasna 132
Baal 51
Bacchantes scandal 30
Balder 50
Baldr 94, 122
Beda venerabilis
  Bede 96
Bede 96
Beelzebub 51
Bellows, Henry Adams 47
Bias of Priene 57
Blavatski, Helena 140
Bohr, Niels 41
Boniface 104
Bormann, Martin 145
Bragi 50
Bragi Boddason 50
Brahma 27
Breker, Arno 145
Brünhild 36
Bultmann, Rudolf 27
Bur 46
Caesar, Gaius Iulius 117
Carmina Burana 131
Chaos 38
Charlemagne 151
Chrestus 32
Cicero 16
Copenhagen interpretation of
  quantum mechanics 41
Council
  of Nicaea 27
Deism 24
Demeter 34
Dionysus 30, 115
do ut des 73
Donar Oak 104
dualism
  heaven-hell 104
  mind-body 91
Elysium 115
Embla 44
Enlightenment 136
Ennead of Heliopolis 42
Eostrae 96
Epicurus 52, 101
Erinyes 52
Eucharist 83
Euhemerus, euhemerism 117
Fafnir 44
Fahrenkrog, Ludwig 148
Fenris Wolf 122, 129
Feuerbach, Ludwig 63
fire-walking 111
Flavius Josephus 32
Flood, the 113, 141
Fólkvangr 94
Forn Sidr 28
Forseti 120
Freyja 94

Frigg 61, 95
Gaia 38
Geirröth 95
Ginnunga-gap 38
Goebbels, Joseph 149
Göring, Hermann 149
Grímnir 95
Grímnismál 95
Grundmann, Walter 150
Gunther 36
Gylfaginning 117
Hades 27, 34
Hagen of Tronje 117
Hagen von Tronje 36
hall of the ancestors 96
Ham 141
hamingja 130
Harner, Michael 86
Harrer, Heinrich 154
Hauer, Jakob Wilhelm 148
Hávamál 98, 101, 118, 125
Heck, Walter 152
Heimdallr 141
Heisenberg, Werner 41
Hel 93, 122
Hephaestus 50
Heracles 44, 58
Hercules Magusanus 60
Hercules's club 111
Hermes 58
Herod 33
Hesiod 108
Himmler, Heinrich 151
Hitler, Adolf 37, 145
Höðr 122
Hœnir 122
Homer 108
Hönir 44
Horaz 136
Horus 27
human sacrifice 76
Hydra 44
Ibn Fadlan 95
iconoclasm 109
Illuyanka 44
Imhotep 50
immanence 49, 90
Indra 44
interpretatio Romana 18
Ishtar 51
Isis 17, 27, 30, 109
Japheth 142
Jarl 141
Jesus 27, 32, 114
Jordan, Wilhelm 43, 46
Jörmungandr 121
Jung, Carl Gustav 55
Juno 27
Jupiter 27, 51
kami 17
Kant, Immanuel 56, 136
Karl 141
Kronos 61
Krucoff, Mitchell W. 85
Kybele 59
Lactantius 15
lares 17
Lemaître, Georges 43
libation 73
Liebenfels, Jörg Lanz von 140
List, Guido von 140
Lodur 44
Loka Táttur 122
Loki 34, 132
Lord Raglan 32, 117
Lucretius 41
Ludendorff, Mathilde 148
Luther, Martin 143
Madsen, Peter 34
magic 84
Mani 61
Mars Thingsus 60
Martell, Karl 156
Mary 109
Meliae 52
Memphis 42
Mercurius Cimbrianus 60
Midgard Serpent 122, 129

Mimir 75
Minerva 27
Minerva-Sulis 141
Mithras 59
Moirai 27
monism 91
Müller, Ludwig 149
multiverse 90
Muspelheim 123
Muspellsheim 38
near death experience 90
neopaganism 135
Nibelungenlied 117
Niflheim 38
Nine Noble Virtues 123
Noah 141
Norns 27, 128
Nun 42
Odin 27, 44, 121
Osiris 27
Ostara 96
Pandeism 24
Panentheism 24
Pantheism 24
Parcae 27
Pascal, Blaise 105
Pascal's Wager 105
penates 17
Pergamon 59
Persephone 34
placebo 82
Pliny, the Younger 50
Pontius Pilate 32
Poseidon 27
Ptah 42
purgatory 100
quantum foam 42, 43
Radbod 96
Ragnarok 20, 42, 130
Rahn, Otto 153
religions
  primary-secondary 22, 155
Rígsmál 141
Rig-Veda 51
Rosenberg, Alfred 156
Röskva 34
Rühmann, Heinz 145
runes 118
Sabazios 116
Sarpedon 20
Satan 32
Saturn 61
Saxnot 60
sea-death 94
Sebottendorf, Rudolf von 140
Seneca 98
Serapis 59
shamanism 86
Shem 141
Shiva 27
Siddhartha Gautama 30
Siegfried 36
Sigurd 44
Simek, Rudolf 31
Simrock, Karl Joseph 46
Sleipnir 122
Snorri Sturloson 116
Speer, Albert 149
spirit journey 86
State church 28
Stauffenberg 37
Steinbock, Fritz 26
Steiner, Rudolf 140
Stoics 98
straw-death 94
Sulis 141
Sundermeier, Theo 22
Sunna 60
Surtr 123
Sveinbjörn Beinteinsson 134
Swastika 144
sword-death 94
Symmachus 137
Tacitus 32, 60
Teiwaz 51
theodicy 108, 121
theoxeny 72
Thjalfi 34

Thor 34, 121
Thor's hammer 111
Thrael (Þræll) 141
Three-Worlds-Theory 53
Tohu wa-bohu 42
transcendence 49
transubstantiation 83
Trimurti 27
Trinity 27
Tyr 51, 120, 123
Uncertainty principle 42
Ussher 20
Valentinian II. 137
Valhalla 93, 95
Vanir 118
Varus 35
Ve 27
Venus 61
Vidar 99
Víðarr 119, 120
Vili 27
Vishnu 27
Völuspá 44
white-coat effect 84
white-coat hypertension 84
Widukind 152
Wiligut, Karl Maria 153
Willibrord 96
Woden 27
Xenophanes 108
Ymir 38
Zeus 27, 51
Ziu 51

Printed in Great Britain
by Amazon